Kingdom Family

Kingdom Family

Re-Envisioning God's Plan for Marriage and Family

TREVECCA OKHOLM

CASCADE *Books* • Eugene, Oregon

KINGDOM FAMILY
Re-Envisioning God's Plan for Marriage and Family

Unless otherwise noted, biblical quotations are taken from the New International Version (NIV) © 1990. Used by permission of Zondervan. www.zondervan.com

Cascade Books
An Imprint of Wipf and Stock Publishers
199 W. 8th Ave., Suite 3
Eugene, OR 97401

www. wipfandstock.com

ISBN 13: 978-1-61097-536-0

Cataloging-in-Publication data:

Okholm, Trevecca.

Kingdom family : re-envisioning God's plan for marriage and family / Trevecca Okholm.

x + 182 p. ; 23 cm. Including bibliographical references.

ISBN 13: 978-1-61097-536-0

1. Families—Religious aspects—Christianity. 2. Church work with families—United States. I. Title.

BV 4526.3 O75 2012

Manufactured in the U.S.A.

To Clara Woods Ganzer,
may you always know that you belong
to God's Kingdom Family

and

To Marian Cross,
our *Faith-Mother* who walked faithfully
and showed us the meaning of hesed hospitality.

Contents

Acknowledgments • *ix*

Introduction • 1

1   *Re-Envisioning the American Dream*: Marriage and Family in Twenty-First Century • 3

2   Missional Living: *Re-Envisioning Community* • 29

3   Identity: *Re-Envisioning Who "I Am"* • 47

4   Direction and Purpose: *Re-Envisioning Marriage, Family, Church, and Kingdom* • 63

5   Learning to "See" Better: *Re-Envisioning our Habits and Disciplines* • 82

6   Freedom in Obedience: *Re-Envisioning Our Response-ability* • 96

7   Desperately Seeking Authenticity: *Re-Envisioning and Re-Membering* • 118

8   Radically Rooted: *Re-Envisioning Stability and Balance in Kingdom Family* • 147

9   Kitchen Community in a Garage Door Society: *Re-Envisioning the Kingdom* • 162

Bibliography • 177

Acknowledgments

I AM indebted to the families of Glen Ellyn Presbyterian Church in Glen Ellyn, Illinois and the families of St. Andrew's Presbyterian Church in Newport Beach, California who have allowed me to walk the journey of faith with them.

Every year that I've practiced ministry has been an adventure in growing my own faith and wishing I'd known how to do it right when I began. Thank you for letting me learn with you and practice on you!

I am indebted to the educators with whom I've shared vision and voice in this journey called Kingdom living. Especially to Diana Garland (whom I've never met, but whose writing has equipped me); to Mark DeVries and Rodney Clapp (both of whom opened my thinking on what it means to be "family" from a Kingdom perspective); to Marva Dawn, Scottie May, Robbie Castleman, and Lib Caldwell (who showed me new ways of welcoming children); to Loretta Gratias-Bremer, Mickie O'Donnell, Nancy Pearson, and Lynn Taylor. And to those who have shown great patience in serving with me in the trenches: Sue Clary, Jan Harvey, Diane Grams, KC Kroeger, Susie Hamlin, Brieana Searcy, Janice Zorn, Pam Gargan, and Diane Johansen.

But most of all, I am grateful beyond words that God allowed me the great gift of serving alongside my husband and best friend, Dennis Okholm, for nearly 40 years—so far—with *never* a dull moment and always a challenge to live up to my potential, serve stronger, live larger, be more faithful, and think better. He has been an encouragement to be and become more of the whole person God created me to be because of our partnership in life and ministry.

Acknowledgments

My desire to live as part of a Kingdom Family, to encourage my own children and grandchildren to live a Kingdom lifestyle that offers so much more than the world could ever imagine, to equip the families in our community of faith to live beyond the cultural expectations and limits—this desire grows stronger each year as I see too many families settle for less that God intends them to be. To see marriages fall apart, to see children suffer from cultural overload and to know that God has a better plan keeps me passionate to make a difference for the Kingdom.

May those who read this book already know that they are called to a higher purpose and a deeper rootedness in the ongoing story of God's Holy people . . . "for once we were not a people, but now we are the people of God."

Introduction

THE KINGDOM AND THE FAMILY

IT WOULD BE A mistake to begin a conversation about living married life and raising children within a Kingdom of God perspective without first having a biblical understating of the Kingdom and a conversation about the meaning of family from a cultural and historical perspective. Therefore, I begin this book with a couple of chapters related to these tasks.

In chapter one I have written briefly on the extensive research that has been done, both from a faith perspective and also from a secular point of view, on the state of marriage and family in our current cultural frame—how we got this way, and what the institution *or deinstitutionalization* of marriage and family at the beginning of the 21st century means for the way we *"do church"* and *"do family"* moving forward.

In chapter two I address the concept of the Kingdom of God and God's call for an alternative way of life by looking at the missional mandate facing many church congregations today. I draw attention to what it means for couples and families who make up the church to begin living missionally, but who often reflect the values of the culture around them better than they are able to reflect the Kingdom of God.

WHY I WROTE THIS BOOK AND
FOR WHOM IT IS WRITTEN

I set out to write for young married couples because of the stress and strain being placed on the institution of marriage in today's world. As my husband, Dennis, and I have often been asked to counsel young college-age couples beginning to explore the possibility of taking on the commitment of married life, and as we've served as a sounding board for young married couples, I've come to realize that there has been very little published on living married life as a "Kingdom" activity—that is, living married life as a means of sanctification and participation in God's plan of redemption.

However, along the way I realized that I had to write this book for families also—for those married couples who have added the holy task of child-rearing to the stress and strain of making marriage work.

Because my professional ministry is primarily to children and their parents, writing about raising children within a Kingdom-focus was appropriate for me and has allowed me to fill chapters three to nine of this book with many practical ideas and stories of training up children in Kingdom-focused faith. I hope that you'll find these chapters equipping, encouraging and practical for your family life.

There is also one more audience that I hope will find this book useful and encouraging: I have written with church leaders in mind.

My desire is to challenge and enlighten Christian educators, pastors, children's pastors, youth ministers, and Christian lay leaders who are trying to understand how the church got so fragmented and age-segregated in the past few decades, and who desire to bring families back to God's original purpose.

I hope you are challenged and encouraged as you read this book.

I hope you will dialogue about it with your spouse and covenant group.

I hope the message of this book will give you pause to think intentionally about how and why you choose to live life as you do.

And I hope and pray that the message of this book will make a difference for the Kingdom of God.

I

Re-Envisioning the American Dream

Marriage and Family in the Twenty-First Century

Some marriages today are miserable not because people are not committed to marriage, but because that is their only commitment.

—William H. Willimon and Stanley Hauerwas

When people evaluated how satisfied they were with their marriages, they began to think more in terms of the development of their own sense of self and the expression of their feelings, as opposed to the satisfaction they gained through building a family and playing the roles of spouse and parent. The result was a transition from the companionate marriage to what we might call the individualized marriage.

—Andrew Cherlin

If the purpose of marriage was simply to enjoy an infatuation and make me happy, then I'd have to get a new marriage every two or three years. But if I really wanted to see God transform me from the inside out, I'd need to concentrate on changing myself rather than on changing my spouse.

—Gary Thomas

WHAT, EXACTLY, IS THE AMERICAN[1]
VERSION OF FAMILY?

And so the story goes: a long time ago, in a galaxy far, far away some beautiful people lived in harmony, in a place called 1950s America—at least that's what we've imagined for the past half century. In reality, 1950s America was the most unusual time for family life in the past century,[2] maybe the most unusual situation for family life since the beginning of recorded history. And, in the past sixty or so years, since our 1950s utopia in suburbia, we have seen the widest pendulum swing in family life in American history.[3]

The mid-twentieth-century nuclear family, which is often touted, especially in evangelical circles, as the "traditional" family and often looked at as the "biblical" model for family, actually has very little in common with the biblical family of the Old and New Testaments. It has more to do with the "Americanization" of family that grew out of our mobility, our quest for independence, the impact of media portrayal of the family with the advent of television, longer life expectancy, and the boon of the post-World War II economy in America.

At the benefit of our North American ethos we find ourselves wrapped into two competing values. One is the value of the perfect, nuclear family and pro-family politics that entice us to idolize marriage as the best way to live one's family life—marriage as a permanent, loving, sexually exclusive relationship, with divorce as a last resort. Our other value embraces the American ethos of rugged individualism and individual rights in which one's primary obligation is to oneself rather than to one's partner and even to one's children. Individuals are encouraged to make choices about the kinds of intimate lives they wish to lead with an increasing quantity of living arrangements that are acceptable,

1. Throughout this book I will use the common term "America" and "Americans" to mean those living in the USA.

2. Cherlin, *Marriage-Go-Round,* 6.

3. Ibid., 8.

and in which folks who are personally dissatisfied with their marriage or other intimate partnership are justified in ending those relationships in favor of personal fulfillment. (In many cases, the ending of these relationships is condoned even by the evangelical church.)

The family in our North American culture has come to symbolize tradition and stability (often in place of historical church traditions) and has come to be thought of as the building-block of community. The nuclear family in America is "inextricably linked with a complex set of moral-political concerns such as male-female roles, children, work and economics and the family is intimately linked in our minds and hearts with our religious faith." The nuclear family has become "a potent symbol of a higher order of life."[4]

In sociological reality, it is interesting to note that American religion as well as civic laws have made room for our national value of individualism by making room for divorce from the earliest years of the nation. At the same time, American-style religion (particularly in post-World War II America) has placed the individual at the center of the religious experience. The Americanization of the church has nurtured the individual's direct relationship with God. As well, the American church structure has tended to divide the family unit of grandparents, parents, youth, and children with a goal to meet individual, age-level needs.

And so we find ourselves at a loss to understand the meaning and purpose of "family" as God intended it to become. We are often conflicted and confused.

Christian families are confronted with conflicting values and purpose, not only from the dramatically transitioning culture, but from our American churches. Too often Christian marriage speakers and counselors promote the "Americanized" version of marriage and family to the exclusion of the gospel message of being members of God's family first.

4. Barton, "Towards a Theology of the Family," 452.

The seed for this book was planted a few years ago when my husband, Dennis, and I were asked to speak at a weekend marriage retreat with newly married couples.

As they listened to us ask the following questions, the young couples seemed a bit confused, and rightly so. The topic we had decided on was what life could be like if Christian couples chose to work toward a more "externally-focused marriage." We began by asking the usual questions:

- What first attracted you to your spouse?

- What increased that attraction as you got to know your future spouse?

But then we began asking them more perplexing questions:

- *Why* did you decide to be a *married* couple?

- How do you react to statements such as: "The church is 'first family,'" "The nuclear family is not God's most important earthly institution,"[5] "The church does not exist to serve the family; the family exists to serve the church." And what do you think Jesus' meant by his statement: "Whoever comes to me and does not hate father and mother, wife and children, brothers and sisters, yes, and even life itself, cannot be my disciple" (Luke 14:26)?

You can probably imagine their perplexity. *No one* ever asks such questions at a *marriage* retreat! We usually think of questions for marriage, particularly in the Christian community, to be more like: How do you love and respect your spouse? How do you embrace the romance? Of course, these are all important questions in creating a close relationship of honor and trust. But, as Gary Thomas asks in the subtitle of his book *Sacred Marriage*,

---

5. Clapp, *Families at the Crossroads*, 67–88.

"What if God designed marriage to make us holy more than to make us happy?"[6]

By the end of that weekend retreat those couples got it—at least, we hoped they did. And in that retreat the seeds for this book were planted. I am writing this book with two groups in mind. First I am writing for the to-be-marrieds, the newly marrieds, the young marrieds just beginning a family, and for parents struggling with the balance of raising Christ-like children in an affluent and often counter-Christian cultural environment.

Second, I am writing this book with the church in mind. My hope is that this book might be discussed by pastors and by teachers, and that it might be of interest for Christian education committees and marriage enrichment teams struggling to equip families to live as faithful members of God's Kingdom in an alien culture.

This book is about living married life and creating a family from a *Kingdom* perspective. What if we were less concerned with insulating ourselves from the culture and more concerned to be a missional[7] model of the God-ordained purpose of our marriage (for the sake of the culture)? This question becomes more urgent when we take a look at the institution of marriage as it stands in the American culture at the beginning of this twenty-first century.

MARRIAGE? NOT "HOW" BUT "WHY"

Why marry? In our American culture that has become the question. There suddenly appears to be a lot of conversation around that question and most of it is not taking place in the Christian community. Of course, the church has a lot to say about how to live well and successfully within marriage and how to raise faith-

6. Thomas, *Sacred Marriage.*

7. I use the terms "missional," "externally-focused" and "Kingdom-focused" interchangeably in this book because all of these define God's call and purpose for His followers.

ful children.[8] However, it appears that today's culture is not so much asking "*How* do we do marriage and family?" as much as it is asking "*Why* should we?"

It is interesting to note that at the same time the establishment and purpose of organized church has come into question. And as we come to grips with the deinstitutionalization of the organized church, the institution of marriage and family is also questioned. From a cultural perspective questions are being asked: What defines marriage? What defines family? Why get married?

Dr. Stephanie Coontz[9] makes a case from history that the idea of marriage for romantic reasons is a fairly new phenomenon. Coontz points out that it has only been in the last hundred years in America that we have put all of our "emotional eggs in the basket of coupled love."[10]

And according to Frances and Joseph Gies, the sociological concept of "family" is a relatively recent development in the history of humanity. In fact, "no European language had a term specifically for the mother-father-children group before the eighteenth century."[11] Marital love and the special relationship between married couple as well as between parents and children— what we now call nuclear families—were simply not considered the basic family unit as they are today. And so, because this is all fairly recent, many of us have found—or at least expected—levels

---

8. There are many useful Christian books and courses on the topic of marriage and family. A few of the most successful are: Parrott, *Becoming the Parent You Want to Be*; Thomas, *Sacred Parenting*; and Castleman, *Parenting in the Pew*.

9. Dr. Stephanie Coontz is the Director of Public Education for the Council on Contemporary Families, Professor of History and Family Studies at Evergreen State College, in Olympia, Washington, and the author of several books on the state of marriage in our culture, including *Marriage, a History: How Love Conquered Marriage*.

10. Coontz, "Too Close for Comfort."

11. Gies, *Marriage and Family in the Middle Ages*.

of pleasure in marriage that our great-great-grandparents never expected to find (despite the romance novels).

We have also put pressures on our marriage partner by neglecting our other relationships, and, according to Coontz, we are "placing too many burdens on a fragile institution and making social life poorer in the process."[12]

By the early twentieth century the sea of change in the culture wrought by the industrial economy had loosened social obligations to neighbors and kin, giving rise to the idea that individuals could meet their deepest needs only through romantic love, culminating in marriage. "The next blow came with the influence of Freud, and society began to view intense same-sex friendships, especially male, with suspicion. Folks were urged to reject the emotional claims of friends and relatives who might compete with a spouse for time and affection."[13]

Coontz goes on to suggest a solution to the pressures put on this modern rendition of marriage, stating that the solution is not to revive what she refers to as "the failed marital experiment of the 1950s," as so many commentators noting the decline in married-couple households seem to want. Nor is it to lower our expectations that we'll find fulfillment and friendship in marriage. Instead, we should raise our expectations for, and commitment to, other relationships, especially since many people now live much of their lives outside marriage. Interestingly, Coontz suggests, we can strengthen our marriages the most by not expecting them to be our sole refuge from the pressures of the world. Instead, "we need to restructure both work and social life so we can reach out and build ties with others, including people who are single or divorced. That indeed would be a return to marital tradition," she says, "not the 1950s model, but the pre-20th-century model that has a much more enduring pedigree."[14]

---

12. Coontz, "Too Close for Comfort."
13. Ibid.
14. Ibid.

CONFRONTING A CULTURE OF DIVORCE
AND SELF-FULFILLMENT

Whether we agree with Coontz or not, we cannot ignore the influence of today's cultural views of marriage if, for no other reason, because statistics show that they have impacted "Christian" marriages nearly to the same extent that all marriages are impacted these days.

Based on a Barna Group study taken among 3,792 adults,[15] statistics show that when evangelical and non-evangelical "born again" Christians are combined into an aggregate class of "born again" adults, their divorce figure is statistically identical to that of non-"born again" adults: 32 percent versus 33 percent, respectively.

"It was a good week for getting divorced," according to *The Week* magazine,[16] "after British department store chain Debenhams launched a gift registry for couples that are calling it quits, so that family and friends can help them begin their new life." And this sort of cultural response reminds me of what David Blankenhorn writes in his book *Fatherless America* as he addresses the fragmentation of marriage and the "culture of divorce" that is pervasive in America in this generation: "Divorce is becoming a metaphor for adult rebirth and renewal."[17]

> The church lives at the intersection of two cultures—a culture of divorce and a culture of permanence, and Christians speak conflicting languages when trying to articulate what they believe. The question is not simply whether divorce is right or wrong, whether it is to be applauded, tolerated or damned. The church's task is not to draw up an eternal list of family do's and don'ts and

15. http://www.barna.org/barna-update/article/15-familykids/42-new-marriage-and-divorce-statistics-released.

16. *The Week*, January 29, 2010, 6.

17. Blankenhorn, *Fatherless America*, 167.

then congratulate itself for being a champion of family values.[18]

Rather, what the church should be asking is,

what must we say to bear witness against shallow and false understandings of marriage in our culture, just as Jesus and Paul bore witness against shallow and false understandings of marriage in theirs? What must we say and do to form our communities so that they bear witness to God's creative intent for the permanent one-flesh union of man and woman in Christ? When these become the framing questions for our normative discourse, we will find creative ways to make the New Testament's witness against divorce speak to our time, just as the New Testament writers found creative ways to make Jesus' teaching against divorce speak to theirs.[19]

Too many Christian marriages have been more influenced by what is happening in marriage and family in culture than they have by God's plan for family. Secular and Christian psychologists and sociologists (and even a few historians) are apprehensive over the state of marriage in our culture today.

On a recent NPR interview with Andrew J. Cherlin, author of *The Marriage-Go-Round: The State of Marriage and the Family in America Today*, the interviewer, Regina Brett, asked how individualism and self-fulfillment have changed traditional American family life.[20] She commented that before couples tie the knot, Cherlin's newest book suggests that they might want to untangle their values. Making a commitment to a spouse so often bumps up against the expectations of an individual's quest for personal self-fulfillment. Why are compatibility and self-fulfillment so often, well, incompatible? On one hand people want to get married and believe they should. On the other hand, they

---

18. Lee, *Beyond Family Values*, 138.

19. Hays, *The Moral Vision of the New Testament*, 373–74.

20. NPR, The Diane Rehm Show, May 28, 2009.

strive for personal happiness and are willing to leave a marriage that no longer provides it.

There are a lot of catchphrases rolling around in the culture these days, phrases such as "culture of divorce" or the "deinstitutionalization of marriage and family."[21] Cherlin, among many other sociologists, tells us that individualized marriage, in which the emphasis is on personal choice and self-development, is expanding not only in our American culture, but also around the world.

When and how did we move from a culture of marriage and family with our vision of 1950's "utopia in suburbia" to a culture of divorce? What does it really mean for our understanding of family and marriage and what marriage has always been known to stand for if we are facing the "deinstitutionalization of marriage"?

In his book, *Families at the Crossroads: Beyond Traditional and Modern Options,* Rodney Clapp writes that in our postmodern world we have put such an emphasis on individuality that we have produced a radical hyper-individualism that emphasizes "the individual over against every collective entity, including the family itself."[22]

The value of hyper-individualism in our culture has been defined in three overlapping moral areas: individual rights, consumerism, and therapy.[23] All three reinforce the logic of cultural individualism by encouraging and mutually reinforcing what have become ideals for Americans: freedom from constraint,

---

21. According to Lee, *Beyond Family Values,* deinstitutionalization is seen as a weakening of the social norms that define people's behavior in a social institution such as marriage. In times of social stability, the taken-for-granted nature of norms allows people to go about their lives without having to question their actions or the actions of others. But when social change produces situations outside the reach of established norms, individuals can no longer rely on shared understandings of how to act. Rather, they must negotiate new ways of acting, a process that is a potential source of conflict and opportunity.

22. Clapp, *Families at the Crossroads,* 24.

23. Ibid., 91.

unlimited opportunity and choice, and self-fulfillment. And we find ourselves living in an era in which the language of individual rights has come to pervade every area of our lives.[24]

It is important for us to look at the state of marriage and family today in light of the biblical implications for our cultural values of individual rights, consumerism, and therapy. However, we also need to look at the impact of other cultural values influencing the way we live and define our relationships. We need to take a look at the impacting value of what Christian Smith and Melinda Denton, in their study of American teens, have called "moralistic therapeutic deism."[25] And, along with individual rights, we also need to consider the insidious value of entitlement, which has a withering effect on the state of marriage and family. As well, we need to address another value, that of busyness which, whether we like it or not, has come to be a sustaining value for Americans today.

INDIVIDUALISM GONE HYPER

"What's in it for me?" has become the mantra for Americans of all ages in the last half century. Music, movies, TV, and especially merchandisers have sold us on our "felt" needs and, even more so, on our "felt" rights. I can still remember the social impact of a commercial for L'Oreal hair color when it was first aired nearly four decades ago. They told me that I would have to pay more for their product but it was certainly okay. Why? "Because I'm worth it!" At that time in culture that was a radical thought; now it seems to be an all too common cultural ethos. A recent article by a London writer, Laura Craik, comments on the influence of the L'Oreal commercial slogan and how it helped to form and change a generation of women to not only believe in themselves, which in theory was a positive step, but also encouraged them to spend what they could not afford in their efforts to seek self worth.

24. Lee, *Beyond Family Values*, 93.
25. Smith and Denton, *Soul Searching*.

"'Why shouldn't I have that?' we think, as our Visa bills ratchet up to the sky. "'Because I'm worth it,'" writes Craik, "might be the best advertising slogan ever penned, but, as a credo for living, it's a bloody disaster."[26] But unfortunately it has become a creed for living and it really is a bloody disaster that defines our American cultural worldview and undermines our relationships.

The impact of this sort of search for value and self-worth has moved from the advertisers to the news media, impacting even the way we communicate news, let alone entertainment. However, the riskiest fallout of advertising and the search for self-worth is the consequence this quest has for our marriages, our families and even our churches. This, I believe, is an important side note that must be mentioned: if our churches and the way we do ministry are impacted by the ethos of personal rights, personal choice, and personal fulfillment, how can we expect our marriages and families to be any different?

Writing on the impact that these cultural values are having on the church in our society today, Princeton cultural sociologist Robert Wuthnow critiques the influx of the popular and personalized "small group" movement and warns that in the midst of all the affirmation for the millions of people involved in small groups, the movement itself is "far too oriented toward individual needs. The formation of small group ministry has become simply a part of an individual's personal 'do-it-yourself' religion that reinforces individualized faith." This has a profound impact on the missional mandate of God's church as well as impacting the families that make up God's church. "The most common reason why people say they join and stay with small groups is what they receive for their own highly personalized needs and goals." The influence of small group ministry in our American churches encourages a "private and inward focused" spirituality that also "permits traditional communities to be abandoned."[27] Or as

26. Craik, "Credit Crunch Shopping."

27. Wuthnow, *Sharing the Journey*, 358. See also, Wuthnow, ed. *"I Come Away Stronger": How Small Groups are Shaping American Religion*. Wuthnow

Southern California pastor Tod Bolsinger puts it, "Culturally we come to think of the church as a dispenser of resources to help the individual on his or her Christian journey. . . . *come here and choose from our wide array of Christian classes, teachings, and activities that you need to live out your individual Christian life.*"[28]

I wonder how we can expect to keep Christian marriages strong when even our Christian journey and our Christian education have become individualized? Many Americans have been trained to become consumers of church and trained to see the church as a *cultural service provider* rather than a community of the faithful living a biblical model of the Kingdom of God.

INDIVIDUAL RIGHTS AND A CULTURE OF ENTITLEMENT

Rights talk has come to pervade every area of our lives and flies in the face of God's Kingdom purpose for marriages and families. "It has become quite natural for us to frame clashes of need or interest in terms of a conflict of rights. Abortion becomes a conflict between the rights of the mother and the rights of the fetus. Child custody often becomes less a decision about what is best for the child and more a battle over the parent's rights. Even litigation on behalf of minor children pits their rights against those of their parents."[29]

This rights talk places us at the center of our moral universe. When we go against the design by which we were created in the

---

described the ethos of the small group as a collection of individuals committed to the group because each of them would say, "I come away stronger."

28. Bolsinger, *It Takes a Church to Raise a Christian*, 16–17 [italics mine]. See also 1 Peter 2:9–10. As Bolsinger writes, "'The church is God's incarnation today. The Church is Jesus' body on earth. The church is the temple of the Spirit. The church is not a helpful thing for my individual spiritual journey. The church is the journey. The church is not a collection of 'soul-winners' all seeking to tell unbelievers 'the Way' to God. The church is the Way. To be part of the church is to be part of God—to be part of God's communion and to be part of God's ministry" (17).

29. Lee, *Beyond Family Values*, 95.

image of God, we put ourselves on the throne and our lives are no longer genuinely, rightly ordered. This creates imbalance in community and possibly more so in marriage and family interactions.

The responsibilities of living in a civil society, in marriage and in family community require mutual and voluntary boundaries to individual freedom. "Freedom in a biblical sense, is not freedom from the demands of others in order to pursue our self-chosen ends, but freedom from the law of sin *in order* to serve God."[30]

As Jesus challenges his followers in John's Gospel: "If you hold to my teaching, you are really my disciple. Then you will know what is true and that truth will set you free" (John 8:31–32).

University of California sociologist Robert Bellah studied the primary commitments and core values of the American people, defining the most cherished and dominant features of our American worldview. Bellah's research found that the two primary commitments of Americans are forms of individualism. He called these two dominant worldviews *Utilitarian Individualism* (If it works for *me*, then it is worthy and good) and *Expressive Individualism* (If it fulfills or satisfies *me*, then it is worthy and good).[31] Interestingly, both of these individualistic worldviews feed into (or, more accurately, are fed by) the defining cultural value in our lives today—consumerism.

The consumer mindset tells us that "if it works for me, then I must have it," and "if it fulfills or satisfies me, then it is worthy of having no matter the cost or implications." Hence the media and the manufacturer sell us what we must have to feed our individualistic worldview. The impact that these two dominant worldviews have on the fragile institutions of modern marriage and family are shattering. Therefore, in less than a decade we in church ministry find ourselves having conversations about how to address a sense of entitlement as a concern in our local congregations and our families (an issue that never seemed to arise

30. Lee, *Beyond Family Values*, 96.
31. Bellah, *Habits of the Heart*.

in my earlier years of ministry). What has caused this to become a prevalent issue for ministry in just the past few years?

The worldviews of utilitarian individualism and expressive individualism (as defined above) have invaded the church community via the families and individuals that make up our congregations, and they directly impact the ways in which we conduct all areas of ministry, from children's education to youth ministry to our corporate worship. We find ourselves working harder to appease the demands of entitled parents and youth who have been culturally trained to consume and expect their individual rights to be accommodated.[32] At the same time that we are often seeking to appease and accommodate, we know full well that this entitlement is not only harming, but also destroying our congregation's marriages and families.

CONSUMER WORLDVIEW

It probably comes as no surprise to anyone that consumerism is pervasive in our culture. It is so hard not to "buy into" (pun intended) this mindset that surrounds our children and us every waking hour. A few years ago I was amazed by the documentary films *Affluenza*[33] and *Merchants of Cool*[34] that factually gave us windows into the influence our consumer culture is having on us and on our children. *Merchants of Cool* documents the ways in which the media markets directly to teens, even creating and changing their felt needs by creating "cool" and then selling it back to teens.

And what is being sold is not so much the products as it is a lifestyle that Americans so desperately want to fit into. It is a way to find our purpose and meaning for life and it keeps us away from being labeled as someone who does not know what's going on, someone who does not fit in. We want this lifestyle, often

32. For more background information on how we got into this situation, see Nelson, *Growing Up Christian*, part 1, as well as Cherlin, *Marriage-Go-Round*.

33. de Graaf, *Affluenza*.

34. Goodman, *Merchants of Cool*.

more for our children than for ourselves. And even we in the church, who call ourselves Christ-followers, are willing to risk our marriages and our families in order to be culturally cool.

Each fall at our church we teach a series of classes on adolescence for fifth graders with parents[35] in order to educate youth, as well as empower parents, about what it means to be created in God's image and about their responsibility to use their bodies, their minds, and their emotions wisely for God's Kingdom purposes.

Our emphasis for the course comes from the writing of the apostle Paul who reminds us, "unlike the culture around you, always dragging you down to its level of immaturity, God brings the best out of you, develops well-formed maturity in you" (Rom 12:1–2, *The Message*).[36] An equally important purpose for the course is to empower and equip the parents of these young adolescents. Parents are required to attend each class session along with their fifth graders. We are very intentional about this so that parents will be learning side by side with their children, and our hope is that even beyond the classes kids will feel more comfortable coming to their parents with questions about anything from hygiene to dating to good decision-making and what God expects of them. On the next-to-last class session we discuss the power and influence of the media and impact of consumerism on our lives. It usually proves to be more of an eye-opening lesson

35. Our curriculum for this St. Andrew's Family Milestone is a partnership between our own materials, *Rites of Passage I* by Dixon www.birdsnbeesconnection.com and James Dobson's *Preparing for Adolescence* curriculum.

36 *The Message* translation articulates the theme verse for our course: "So here's what I want you to do, God helping you: Take your everyday, ordinary life—your sleeping, eating, going-to-work, and walking-around life—and place it before God as an offering. Embracing what God does for you is the best thing you can do for him. Don't become so well-adjusted to your culture that you fit into it without even thinking. Instead, fix your attention on God. You'll be changed from the inside out. Readily recognize what he wants from you, and quickly respond to it. Unlike the culture around you, always dragging you down to its level of immaturity, God brings the best out of you, develops well-formed maturity in you" (Rom 12:1–2).

for the parents (especially the moms) than for the girls or boys. Why is it that we are so easily "sold"?

Consumerism is one of the main causes for the culture of divorce that has been created in our American culture; even our Christian subculture is not immune. Mammon is a powerful god to serve, and the power of acquiring "stuff" seems so fulfilling. Why is it so much easier to spend four hours at a mall than two hours worshiping or doing acts of service with our spouse or with our children? What damage this drive to possess does to our marriages and to our parenting possibilities.

We know that we want to raise our kids free from the power of media and affluence, free from the power of cool, but the draw is so strong to fit in, to be a part of, to feel included that it forms us even as we are willfully trying to resist.

When our nation was more of an agricultural and industrial civilization, families were able to handle the pressures of consumption more because there was no media influence constantly telling us what we need, what we want, and what we must have. But it is important also to point out that we have arrived at this situation due to the fact that families in our culture rarely produce together; their common bond is lowered to what they consume together instead. I will talk more about this in a later chapter where I address the powerful bond and enriched experience that comes from families finding a purpose beyond themselves. The practice of producing together versus only consuming together strengthens not only our culture and our community as a means of giving back and serving, it also strengthens and binds our families together into a higher calling than just ourselves, our felt needs and our entitlement.

THERAPY AND MORALISTIC THERAPEUTIC DEISM: I GET BY WITH A LITTLE HELP FROM MY GOD

Complementing the stressors of individual rights and consumerism on our marriages, families and community, there is another cultural condition that has the power to draw us into a lifestyle of fear and dependency. That is the power of a therapeutic view of God and the church—the view that God exists not only to meet my needs, but to fix me and make me feel completed and happy. Therapy, of course, can be very health giving for individuals, for marriages, and for families. So please don't misunderstand the fact that in many instances it is therapy, particularly Christian therapy, that offers realignment and right-ordering of our decisions, our actions, and our emotions. However, there is a danger that is insidious in our culture that creates an underlying sense of *fear*. An underlying fear of what is, of what was and what it has done to me and to my children, and fear of what might be missing in my life may cause a dependency on therapy. We will talk more about this at the end of the chapter when we discuss our basic human needs. However, more to the point of our cultural worldview in the past half-century is this other type of "therapy" impacting our marriages and our families today. It is what we have already referred to as *Moralistic Therapeutic Deism*, a way in which many in our society have come to visualize God.

In their book and subsequent DVD documentary, *Soul Searching: The Religious and Spiritual Lives of American Teenagers*, Christian Smith and Melinda Lundquist Denton address a view of God and religion held by a large number of the teens that they interviewed for their book and documentary. They describe this view of God as "Moralistic Therapeutic Deism." It is a religion that is, as the label indicates, first and foremost deeply moralistic.

According to the average American, the moral of the human story is to pursue the good of being happy. Therefore, the average American believes that this fulfillment of happiness comes to the nice and the kind, the pleasant and the self-motivated. As such MTD is a deeply inclusivist religion, since all religions share this concern for the good, moral life. In addition to a basic moralism, though, MTD is also humanitarian. It is concerned for well being, and, most importantly, this well being is typically understood in therapeutic terms. The problems of life, many Americans apparently believe, "have little or nothing to do with sin, but with subjective wellness. In light of the surveys they conducted," the authors interestingly link the fact that "most teens are religiously inarticulate" to their common faith in the quest to feel happy.[37] The ambiguities of personal subjectivity ("it just makes me feel good") too often inhibit the Church's traditional concern for a believer's clear confession of faith. And, rather naturally, this leads to the third feature of MTD: it is idolatrous, having substituted a false God for the true God. "Moralistic Therapeutic Deism," the authors write, "is a belief in a particular kind of god: one who exists, created the world, and defines our general moral order, but not one who is particularly personally involved in my daily affairs—especially affairs in which one would prefer not to have God involved. Most of the time, the God of this faith keeps a safe distance."[38]

Another therapeutic-based issue that arises from MTD is the drive American parents have to build a sense of self-esteem in their children—a mindset that feeds into individualism and is fed by consumerism.

Po Bronson and Ashley Merryman write about this drive to build self-esteem in a chapter on the "Inverse Power of Praise" in their book *NurtureShock: New Thinking About Children.* They cite the statistic that between 1970 and 2000 there were over 15,000 scholarly articles written on self-esteem and its relationship to everything from sex to career advancement.[39] Not a surprise, of course, if you walked the aisles of most bookstores or libraries in that era. However, what is somewhat surprising is that the *results were often contradictory or inconclusive.*

In 2003 the Association for Psychological Science asked Dr. Roy Baumeister, then a leading proponent of self-esteem, to review much of the self-esteem literature. His team concluded that self-esteem research was polluted with flawed science. Most of those 15,000 studies asked people to rate their self-esteem

37. Smith and Denton, *Soul Searching*, 164.
38. Ibid.
39. Bronson and Merryman, *NurtureShock,* 18.

and then asked them to rate their own intelligence, career success, relationship skills, and so forth. "These self-reports were extremely unreliable since people with high self-esteem have an inflated perception of their abilities. Only 200 of the studies employed a scientifically sound way to measure self-esteem and its outcomes."[40]

> After reviewing those 200 studies, Dr. Baumeister concluded that having high self-esteem did not improve grades or career achievement. It didn't even reduce alcohol usage. And it especially did not lower violence of any sort. (Highly aggressive, violent people happen to think very highly of themselves, debunking the theory that people are aggressive to make up for low self-esteem.) At the time, Baumeister was quoted as saying that his findings were "the biggest disappointment of my career."[41]

Baumeister is now on the other side of the argument. He recently published an article showing that for college students on the verge of failing in class, esteem-building praise causes their grades to sink further. Baumeister has come to believe that continued appeal of self-esteem is largely tied to a parent's pride in their children's achievements; it's so strong that "when they praise their kids, it's not that far from praising themselves."[42]

Might it be that offering praise has become a style of therapy for the anxieties of modern parenting? Reading Bronson's and Merryman's chapter on the inverse power of praise unpacks the myriad ways in which a parent's efforts to build a child's character with praise can backfire.

40. Ibid.
41. Ibid., 19.
42. Ibid.

BUSYNESS AND RESTLESSNESS: AND I STILL HAVEN'T FOUND WHAT I'M LOOKING FOR

I know a person who is semi-retired, in his late 70s, and should have "earned the right" to be reveling in more leisure time and appreciating (as well as reflecting on) a long life, well-lived. However, he usually begins every phone conversation by telling us how busy he is. He complains of no time to relax—so many demands on him. He just seems consumed with letting us know that he is *busy*. My husband and I conclude that he is afraid that if he is not busy (or at least if he cannot convince himself he is busy), he feels that he has little value in life. Apparently, to *admit* that one is relaxing or taking time to reflect on life or reading a book (or even taking a nap) is to admit that one is not all that important to the world.

This frenetic busyness unfortunately even impacts our ability to read and dwell in the Holy Scriptures and do Bible study. An unspoken equation is that busyness equals importance and success. And my friend is not an isolated case. We all succumb to the desire to prove our value by how busy we can appear to others as well as to ourselves. We also succumb to the pressure to prove our children's worth by how many activities they are involved in and how busy their lives are, fearing that they may miss something of value to their personal growth and development without constant busyness.

What is the impact of this busyness on the state of marriage and family? One of the main impacts is that of stress and unhealthy tension. If we take the fragile state of marriage with the pressures addressed by Stephanie Coontz at the beginning of this chapter—namely, that the expectation of marriage in our culture is that of our sole refuge from the pressures of the modern work force—and add to it those daily pressures that keep our lives in a constant state of hurry and restlessness as we seek after the next best thing, it is no wonder that our marriages and families are failing. At the very moment that we want it all, it is slipping between our fingers.

Stephen Covey writes about this felt pressure in his time management matrix,[43] in which he says we risk the "important but not urgent" for the sake of the "urgent but unimportant" in our lives and even in our families.

Bronson and Merryman address this in another way in their book *Nurtureshock*. They cite statistics that show that children get one hour less sleep now at the beginning of the twenty-first century than they did thirty years ago. Sleep, they tell us, is a biological imperative for every species on earth. "But humans alone try to resist its pull. Instead, we see sleep not as a physical need but a statement of character. It is considered a sign of weakness to admit fatigue—and it is a sign of strength to refuse to succumb to slumber. Sleep, it seems, is for wusses."[44]

As I've implied, another word for busyness in this context is restlessness. Restlessness permeates our culture. We are always seeking after the next thrill, the next important discovery, the next way to keep ourselves entertained. We flip on the TV or iPod as soon as we enter a room. We incessantly check e-mail and Facebook for fear we might miss something or be left out. The desire to be entertained and connected fuels our restlessness. Yet, this condition of restlessness is nothing new. Sixteen centuries ago, St. Augustine commented on our human state of restlessness when he wrote "our hearts are restless until they find their rest in God." And even as we seek God we are restless. Even to be still and quiet in our worship makes most folks twitch.

We simply cannot have down time or quiet in daily lives. Even our worship must be filled with words or music or movement. It almost seems that we're afraid to be quiet. Although we know that the Psalmist reminds us to "be still and know that God is God" (Psalm 46:10) we have difficulty in the practice of coming into a holy-other presence in quiet, silent, focused reflection.

In a recent sermon our pastor talked about a cultural condition referred to as continuous partial attention (CPA). We can

43. Covey, *First Things First*.
44. Bronson & Merryman. *NurtureShock*, 43–44.

chuckle that we're all victims of CPA with the overload of media and our fear of missing out on something. However, in reality that pervasive need to be so connected to everything that we give full attention to nothing of sustaining value hits too close to home. Our value of busyness and the need to stay connected is manifested in our inability to be quiet, reflective, peaceful, focused, and committed either to our marriages and families or to our God.

This busyness and restlessness is fed by our values of consumerism and therapy. If only I *could* or If only I *was* or If only I *had*: it all fuels our lack of stability in our relationships. In what way might a Christian marriage be an example of contentment and peace and stability in a world full of people who still haven't found what they're looking for? What would it take to get there?

It often seems that our modern economy is based on the multiplication of activities and pleasures and increasingly time-consuming tasks, all of which compete to take our minds off God and his agenda. God calls us to join him in the work of bringing in his Kingdom "on earth as it is in Heaven." While our culture tells us to enjoy as much as we possibly can squeeze in, the Lord says, "Be still . . . and know . . . that I Am God" (Psalm 46:10). Christ calls us not to consume or seek therapy or stand up for our rights. His calls us to be His disciples, so that we will know the Truth that will set us free (John 8:31–32).

WHO AM I? . . . WHY AM I HERE? . . . WHERE AM I GOING?

In one of the Kingdom parables in Matthew, Jesus tells the story of a merchant who searched high and low for a pearl of great worth, and when he found that pearl he was able to recognize its worth and was willing to give up everything he owned just to possess it. What could be so valuable? Of course, we know that Jesus was talking about the Kingdom of God. Yet here we are, seeking after so many things to fill our needs, to give us our worth, to capture the American dream, that we look just beyond that pearl of great worth in case there is something better to be had.

Several years ago I attended an Association of Presbyterian Church Educator's convention when it was being hosted in Chicago. A message that has remained with me from that convention was at the end of a workshop led by author and theologian Marva Dawn. In the Q&A time at the end someone asked a question about how to speak and teach so that different generations (particularly the younger generations) would be reached with the truth. Marva gave what seemed to me a profound answer—an answer that has influenced my ministry with families over the years. She said that although different generations have different modes of communication and different experiences and interests, the bottom line is that every person in every generation from the beginning of time has seven basic needs. If those needs are addressed and met then people will be fulfilled and emotionally healthy. We all strive for these seven basic human needs:

1. A sense of *identity* (Who am I?)

2. A *meta-narrative* (Do I belong to a bigger story?)

3. A *community* (What is my place? To whom am I accountable?)

4. A sense of *purpose* (Why am I here? What is my worth?)

5. *Values* (What defines my way of life? What are my rituals? What are my traditions?)

6. A sense of *direction* (Where am I going?)

7. A sense of *power* and *hope* (Can I survive? Who or what is in control of my destiny?)

Being real and committed participants in God's Kingdom puts us in a right position to recognize, receive, and to even pass on the parable's pearl of great worth. Participating in God's Kingdom gives us an identity—a purpose beyond ourselves. Knowing the history of God's faithfulness to his people down through time and recognizing prophecies fulfilled fits us in God's community, realigns our values, and puts our lives into a meta-narrative that gives power, hope, and direction.

Our Christian families are filled with restless hearts seeking after something and someone to give them identity, meaning, direction, power, and hope. In the next few chapters I will give some practical suggestions for ways that Christian couples can encourage each other in a Kingdom perspective and parents can help their children gain a Kingdom identity that is bigger and deeper than the identity of an individual family of origin. Even though our identity within our family tree is also necessary in establishing a sense of worth, there is a deeper identity that our hearts are restless to embrace.

CONVERSATION STARTERS

For engaged couples and newly married couples:

1. In what ways do you see some of the cultural values already making demands on your relationship?

   - Individual rights or entitlement?

   - Consumerism?

   - Busyness?

2. As you plan for your future together (possibly with children), how might you intentionally plan to give yourself and your family a sense of identity and direction? What will define your life story?

For families with children:

1. How do you see your family life being impacted by some of the cultural values so prevalent in our North American worldview? How do you think you might begin to redirect these influences in your home?

---

2. As you read further chapters in this book you will discover biblical stories and examples to assist you in your goals. Are there some already on your mind?

For Christian educators, pastors, and education committees:

1. In what ways do you address meeting these seven basic human needs when planning curriculum and programming in your church? Do you agree or disagree that this is important for strengthening marriages and families in your congregation?

2. Have you considered adding ministry that helps folks wrestle with many of the cultural values that define us more completely than God's message of an alternative, Kingdom-focused lifestyle?

2

Missional Living

Re-Envisioning Community

———◦•◦———

Gated communities are growing faster than ghettos.

—Ray Bakke

As increasing numbers of families continue to be fractured and fragmented, Christ-centered families will stand out more and more as outposts of light in neighborhoods of darkness.

—Jay Strother

As we grow in our love, as we grow in our calling as a couple, we are better equipped to be the presence of Christ in the lives of those around us. Being the presence of Christ in the world moves us toward the missional model for our families.

—Bo Prosser

MARRIAGE AND FAMILY FOCUSED ON GOD'S KINGDOM

"WHAT IS GOD'S KINGDOM?" That's a question that I asked a group of elementary-age children at my church. As we talked about the topic of the Kingdom, we wondered together about the words of our "Lord's Prayer," which say, "Thy *Kingdom* come, thy *will* be done." We wondered together about when, where, and how this Kingdom and God's will is supposed to "come and be done on earth *just like* it is in Heaven."

I asked the children to think about what it's like for us to be citizens of the United States of America? Answer: we pay taxes, we vote, we have a government that runs things (even if it is not always perfect and we complain about it!), we have schools and places of beauty to enjoy, such as National Parks and beaches. But the most important thing about being a citizen is that we know we belong and we know we are called to serve and respect our nation. Then I helped the children to think about the Kingdom of God as a nation—a nation that is in this world (like all other nations on earth), but not *of* this world.

Throughout both the Old and New Testaments the Kingdom of God is a recurring theme. The prophets such as Isaiah, Jeremiah, and Daniel spoke of God's eternal Kingdom (see Isa 9:6–7; Jer 10:7; Dan 4:3). However, this is even more the case in the Gospels and the earthly ministry of Jesus, where we see that the central theme of all Jesus' teaching and work is the Kingdom of God. In fact, note the first recorded words of Jesus in his public ministry as recorded in Mark 1:15: "The time has come, the Kingdom of God is near." (Or as Eugene Peterson translates it in *The Message:* "Time's up! God's Kingdom is here. Change your life and believe the message." See also Luke 4:43 and 8:1).

John the Baptist also foretold the coming of the Kingdom of God (Matt 3:2). In fact, John the Baptist was the last voice and last member of the long line of prophets who announced the coming Kingdom.

Several of the parables Jesus taught were ways of explaining the Kingdom in images the people might begin to understand. I love to tell those parables to children and plant the seeds of wonder in their hearts and minds: "I wonder what sort of pearl is so valuable that the person would be willing to sell everything they own just to receive it?" "I wonder what this tiny mustard seed might really be and I wonder what makes it grow big enough to make a home for all the birds of the air to come and nest in its branches? I wonder what that tree might really be? I wonder if that tree might be big enough for all the people of the world to come and make a home in its branches?"[1]

The Kingdom of God is the rule of an eternally sovereign God who reigns over all creatures and all things (Ps 103:19; Dan 4:3). The Kingdom of God embraces all created intelligences, both in heaven and on earth, that are in fellowship with God and are *willingly subject* to God's authority.

The Kingdom is not so much a place or territory as it is the reign or rule of God in the lives and affairs of humans. The Kingdom of God is where the will of God is done (Matt 6:10). The Kingdom of God is the reign of God in human history through Jesus Christ (Luke 4:16–22; Matt 12:22–29), the purpose of which is to redeem God's people from sin and demonic powers, and finally to establish a new heaven and new earth. God is the ruler and authority over the entire created universe, and he is acting in history to bring it to its divine goal. The ultimate goal is cosmic redemption (Eph 1:9–10; Col 1:19–20; Rom 8:19–21).

We enter the Kingdom when we come to faith in Jesus Christ as savior of our life; we participate in the Kingdom as we continually (often on a daily basis) invite Jesus Christ to be the Lord of our lives. We enter by God's grace as we continue the daily practice of surrendering our will to God's purpose.

When I talk with the children in our community about being citizens of the Kingdom of God, I want to help them understand that we not only belong as citizens of the United States of America with all the rights and responsibilities of being called Americans, but as children of God in the church we belong as citizens of God's Kingdom with all the rights and responsibilities of being called Christians.[2]

---

1. This model of teaching the parables with "wondering" questions is developed in Stewart and Berryman, *Young Children in Worship.*

2. I actually try to use the term "followers of God" when talking with

I try to help our children get it because so many of the "churched" adults when asked "What is the Kingdom of God?" will answer that it is somewhere out there and that it requires nothing more of them than a declaration of faith, the act of baptism, and an assurance (or insurance) for their after-life. And when many teens and adults living with a moralistic, therapeutic deistic view of God[3] they are less likely to become true followers of Jesus Christ and participate in his Kingdom work here on earth.

Part of the responsibility and privilege of being a follower of Jesus Christ is building for God's reign here on earth "just as it is in Heaven." But somewhere along the line we have inadvertently become better citizens of an earthly nation than fully committed citizens of the Kingdom of God. Not only that, but we have done a better job of educating and indoctrinating our children to be good citizens of secular nations than Kingdom-belonging citizens of God.

THERAPY AS MINISTRY, OR THE CONFESSIONS OF A SOCIOLOGY MAJOR

It is interesting to note that in the past few decades many of our American churches actively looked to the social sciences for models of family ministry: "Many of the ministry leaders who are shaping church programs today came of age in graduate school during the 1960s and 1970s when there was an explosion of study in mental health and social sciences, and they have translated this model to the church."[4]

I can attest to this, having received my undergraduate degree in the study of sociology in the early '70s from an evangelical institution. This was at a time when the Christian study of

children due to the negative cultural connotations often associated with "Christian" in our world; besides, "follower of God" more aptly communicates the concept of discipleship.

3. Smith and Denton, *Soul Searching*, 30–71.

4. Garland, *Family Ministry*, 299.

sociology and psychology were two of the most popular majors on college campuses. We learned in theory how to "do religion" within a framework of sociology and psychology.

The church's ministry with families in the past few decades in America has inadvertently been shaped according to the community mental health model. The danger in this is that the church has promoted therapy as ministry. The primary goal of such ministry is to prevent problems by providing support services and educational programs which, in and of themselves, are very important and worthwhile. However, "churches are not community health centers."[5] No church can meet all the needs, even for educational services and counseling, within its own membership, much less in the larger community. It also seems that these programs, as beneficial as they may be, are often too little too late. As Diana Garland puts it: "They do not cut to the heart of the social forces that besiege families today. This is where the community mental health model fails the church. And this model with its community needs assessment cannot be the *starting point* for building Godly families."[6]

A MISSIONAL INROAD FOR GOD'S KINGDOM

It is important to note that the church in the American culture has also been defined within a concept of the modern and postmodern worldview. As well, we have seen the influences of individualism, consumerism, moralistic therapeutic deism, and busyness as the foundation of the disillusionment over organized religion. It is in response to this cultural framing of the way to do religion that some Christian leaders are now calling for the church to move back to its biblical mandate to become salt and light in the culture. The call for the church is to become a missional outpost for God's Kingdom.

5. Ibid.
6. Ibid., 300.

In order for the church to be missional, we must look for practical ways in which marriage and the family might be called back into a God-ordained, biblical purpose. Not the 1950s idealistic marriage and family of the modern age nor the 1800s Victorian, romanticized family, but family formed and functioning according to the biblical mandate to be a model of Christ's holiness—marriage and family functioning within a "citizen of God's Kingdom" perspective.

So much of what we see and read in Christian literature for marriage is inwardly focused—so inwardly focused that a kind of marital narcissism sets in. Christ followers are called to live in Kingdom-focused marriages, not modeled after the secular culture or as an escape *from* the secular culture, but as a model of God's faithfulness and plan for the world.

Perhaps if we accepted the calling to marriages that are externally focused as missional outposts for God's work in the world and looked seriously at what the Bible has to say about marriage, and more specifically what Jesus had to say about marriage, we might need to tweak our concept of what marriage, or at least our concept of *Christian* marriage, is all about. How does our marriage and our family make a Kingdom statement to the world?

As we talk about Kingdom-focused marriage, we must also think about what it means to raise children with a missional attitude and Kingdom calling of God. Who are these small demanding strangers that come into our homes and what is our privilege and responsibility to participate with them in God's Kingdom purposes for this world? Steve Kang puts it this way in an article he wrote on Christian parenting:

> Our earthly children are also our brothers, sisters, and friends with whom we practice mutual encouragement, forgiveness, submission, and love in all our ways. As we practice the life of loving God completely, ourselves accurately, and others compassionately, we fulfill our calling as God's children, particularly as parents, in inviting

our children to participate in the earthly embodiment of God's [Kingdom] together.[7]

Last summer my husband and I joined a team of lay people on a summer mission to the African nation of Uganda. Among this fourteen-person team we had two young women who just completed their freshman year at two different colleges. We also had a young woman who had just completed her freshman year in high school. These three did not know each other before joining our team, but they all three had something very important in common. First of all, two of them were traveling for the first time without their families. However, all three families had modeled and made missional lifestyle a priority that influenced the choices their daughters were making. Each one had already traveled on short-term mission services with her parents several times, so that missional living became a lifestyle for all three. I know that their caring and service and participation in God's Kingdom work at home and around the world will continue as they move into adulthood. The families of these young women have moved beyond sending their children on spring break mission trips, taking them into lifestyle mission as partners and, as Kang says above, "inviting [their] children to participate in the earthly embodiment of God's [Kingdom] together."

TO TELL THE TRUTH . . . WE MUST LIVE THE TRUTH

In their book, *The Externally Focused Church*, Rick Rusaw and Eric Swanson begin with an explanation of where the church currently is located in our culture and why it makes sense for us to begin thinking, living and doing church within a more externally-focused, missional perspective.[8] Their statistics tell us that the church in America today is becoming more and more marginalized and less and less influential. I would add that as

---

7. Kang, "When Our Children Become Our Brothers, Sisters, and Friends in God's Household," 14.

8. Rusaw and Swanson, *Externally Focused Church*, 11.

the influence of the church in America goes, so goes Christian marriage and family. Whereas just a few decades ago the typical church-going family was perceived as the norm and model for the America ideal, that same idealized family is becoming not only marginalized but also portrayed negatively in media. As Rusaw and Swanson remind us, "We don't need another Barna study to tell us that fewer people feel the church can help them."[9]

To tell the truth of God's Kingdom we must practice habits that show the truth of God's Kingdom. The proponents of externally-focused or missional church models remind us of this fact.[10] We need to begin to think about what habits can be intentionally practiced in our marriage and family that will show the culture the truth of God's Kingdom.

According to Rusaw and Swanson, externally-focused churches are defined in the following ways:

1. They are inwardly strong but outwardly focused.

2. They integrate good deeds and good news into the life of the church.

3. They value impact and influence in the community more than attendance.

4. They seek to be salt, light, and leaven in the community.

5. They see themselves as the "soul" of the community.

6. They would be greatly missed by the community if they left.

The same characteristics should define Christian marriages. And for families, we need to consider how marriages and families can grow inwardly strong but outwardly focused, growing by doing and existing the way that God commands in his Word. We have this mandate: to integrate good deeds and good news into the life of our church and the lives of our families that make up the church.

9. Ibid.
10. Ibid., 12.

Kingdom-focused families must learn to value the impact and influence they can have in their community. Perhaps we need to consider what it looks like to be involved in God's mission beyond weekly (or monthly) church attendance.

Missional families are made up of people who seek to be salt, light, and leaven in their communities, and missional parents seek to bring salt, light, and leaven into the ways in which they nurture their children to be worthy citizens of God's Kingdom. Do we see our marriages and our families as the soul of the community? It should be possible to think of ourselves as God's best hope for the community both within the church as well as within our local neighborhoods. How might we lead lives that reveal God's goodness as an alternative to the cultural ethos?

Is it possible that our families would be greatly missed by the community if they left? I often tell our church's children and families that they can make a difference in their world. But, instead, Christian families too often choose to do one of these two things: they either choose to insulate and isolate from the culture or, more likely, Christian families model the same values in lifestyle as the culture around them rather than modeling God's Kingdom purposes.

RADICALLY MISSIONAL

Not long ago our daughter, Emily, introduced us to an interesting blogspot that was created by a young family seeking to live their marriage and raise their children with a focus on God's Kingdom.[11] While reading their blogspot, I came across a post reflecting on the February 2009 issue of *Christianity Today* that featured an article by Mike Barrett titled, "Searching for Radical Faith." In it, Barrett talks about traveling around the world to find radical Christians.

---

11. www.leaderchick.blogspot.com. There are many such sites springing up in the past few months including: www.aholyexperience.com and www.watkinseveryflavorbean.blogspot.com.

Barrett said that he expected to find radical Christians among tattooed snowboarders for Christ, in-your-face protesters, or polarizing public figures. Instead, he found that true radicals look "downright ordinary," and certainly do not try to draw attention to themselves. He found "quiet nuns, home-schooling moms, church planters, and lifelong missionaries, toiling in obscurity in cultures hostile to the gospel, but in desperate need of it."

> I had been tricked into thinking that radicals were somehow flashy, famous, and dangerous, but they're not. They're just not. True radicals are quietly praying and fasting for the sick in their church. They're taking in foster children. They're taking seriously Christ's words, "If anyone would come after me, let him deny himself, pick up his cross, and follow me." The problem is that Jesus' call isn't just for a few heroes. We prefer the "radical" that rides a motorcycle, writes edgy books, does podcasts, speaks at conferences (for top fees), and never really sacrifices much at all. But we're swallowing a placebo, a sugar pill that claims to make life more interesting.[12]

Families like the ones writing such missional family blogs are at the forefront of a movement to model their marriage and family life after Christ and his church. There are many other examples of Christian couples striving to become more missional and Kingdom focused. Families such as these force us to ask ourselves: How intentional are our Christian marriages and families in living beyond ourselves in order to be faithful to God's Kingdom purpose for the world?

On another missionally focused website, www.gospelcom .net, Ray Bakke states, "Gated communities are growing faster than ghettos." The model of some Christian families in the past few decades seems to have been to try to "escape the culture by retreating to the culturally perceived ideal communities of suburbia, to private schools and to exclusive clubs. We fantasize about

12. Barrett, "Searching for Radical Faith."

our safety and retreat into isolation. Yet, all the while, we wish so desperately to belong in real community." [13] According to Bakke,

> The missional family rejects this exclusivity and chooses instead to join in the real world. The missional family brings the presence of Christ into public schools, into the inner city, into places where [Kingdom] ministry might flourish. The missional family is not repulsed by misfortune, poverty or disease but rather, it readily responds as Jesus would respond with love and compassion. [14]

What might it mean for our culture to be exposed to missional or Kingdom-focused marriages? This is a new idea diverging from what has been touted as the "traditional" Christian family of the 50s and beyond. Where do Kingdom-seeking marriages and families go for guidance in living missionally?

WOEFULLY UNPREPARED

Too many people who claim the distinction of Christian in our American culture are woefully unprepared to live out the faith they claim to believe, let alone communicate it to a longing world. They know too little of God's story, too little biblical teaching, and too little of God's moral framework to exemplify and testify to their faith. They blend into the culture, try to escape the culture, or are overwhelmed by the culture; some are constantly faith-shopping in search of a newer option that will be therapy for their felt needs.

Christians, just like anyone else living under the ethos of the American Dream, are after quick fixes, simple answers—three ways to get your spouse to communicate better, five steps to a more exciting love life, and quick answers for a happier marriage. Gary Thomas puts it this way in his book *Sacred Marriage*:

> We can use the challenges, joys, struggles, and celebrations of marriage to draw closer to God and to grow in

13. Bakke, http://cityvoices.gospelcom.net/pages/raybakke/ray_apstle.html.
14. Ibid.

Christian character. But first we have to rid ourselves of the notion that the difficulties of marriage can be overcome if we simply pray harder or learn a few simple principles. Most of us have discovered that these 'simple steps' work only on a superficial level. Why is this? Because there's a deeper question that needs to be addressed beyond how we can "improve" our marriage: *What if God didn't design marriage to be "easier"? What if God had an end in mind that went beyond our happiness, our comfort, and our desire to be infatuated and happy as if the world were a perfect place? What if God designed marriage to make us holy more than to make us happy?* What if we are to accept the "bitter juice" because out of it we may learn to draw the resources we need with which to make "the honey of a holy life"?[15]

THE GREAT HUMAN PROJECT OF HOLY MATRIMONY: A SACRAMENTAL VIEW OF MARRIAGE

From a Reformed perspective I understand a sacrament to be a sacred action that reflects the power, purpose, and participation of God in our church community. In the Presbyterian Church we have only two sacraments: baptism and communion. I teach our church's children and parents that we have these two because they are the only sacraments specifically mandated in the New Testament (as Calvin taught, rightly or wrongly). However, in the Catholic Church there are seven sacraments, and one of those involves a sacramental view of marriage.

As a sacrament in the Catholic Church as well as a covenant promise in the Protestant faith, marriage is to be a sign of the covenant faithfulness that God keeps with his people Israel as he calls them to be the instrument through which he will bless all the nations.

The biblical story of the prophet Hosea is a beautiful depiction of God's *hesed*[16] (faithfulness) in this marriage. And, now,

---

15. Thomas, *Sacred Marriage*, 12 (italics mine).

16. The Hebrew word *hesed* does not have a comparable translation in

by extension, the church, as the bride of Christ (Eph 5), is to be signified in our Christian marriages.

David Thomas' book, *Christian Marriage: The New Challenge*, helps us to understand Catholic marriage as a holy sacrament. He writes that "God invites us in on the great human project through creating a social reality that unites woman with man for the whole of life. This involves a joining of persons for their own sake and for the sake of those that their life will touch."[17]

That understanding of the holiness of marriage is certainly in keeping with the models used in Scripture—that of marriage as a union which represents God's relationship to Israel in the Old Testament and Christ's relationship to his church in the New Testament. How meaningful it should be to stand before a couple in the bonds of marriage and remind them that they are entering into a *great human project* that involves not only joining together for their own sake, but also as a witness to all those whose lives they'll be touching over their lifetime together—including any children they may nurture.

In our culture today we simply do not make enough of *holy* matrimony! The act of coming together to form and be formed as a witness to faithfulness in our world is a model our world is desperately seeking; however, when Christians take cultural cues for the ways they live life together and raise children we are going on an adventure in missing the point.

The essence of holy matrimony is a true and enduring participation in God's community, a foretaste of heavenly community, the essence of effective discipleship, and an enduring witness to an unbelieving world. In talking about the call to faithfulness in marriage, Stanley Hauerwas and William Willimon write:

> Christians who are called to marriage are called to practice lifetime, exclusive, monogamous fidelity. Christians

English, but it is best defined by the actions of some of our faith ancestors in the Old Testament, such as the prophet Hosea's actions toward his unfaithful wife, Gomer, and the actions of Boaz toward Ruth.

17. Thomas, *Christian Marriage*, 124.

who remain single are called to support marriage. Any debate about divorce or remarriage after divorce must take place against the background of this command and the community it envisions. In mainline Protestantism, we have not really debated divorce and remarriage against the background of our beliefs about God, other than a sentimental notion of "grace." What we have done is simply to leave such decisions to the private consciences of people, and as a result we have abandoned people to their own self-deceit or to enslavement by a consumerist culture.[18]

AN ALTERNATIVE CULTURE VERSUS AN ACCOMMODATING CULTURE

Just as Jesus called his first disciples to be an alternative culture rather than accommodate to the prevailing culture, the time has come for North American Christians to take a close look at how the church is being influenced and formed by the culture that surrounds them and ask, Where do we go from here if we are not in nineteenth-century "Christian America" anymore nor the mid-twentieth-century "ideal" American nuclear-family? The answer that Hauerwas and Willimon give is worth quoting at length:

> Some marriages today are miserable not because people are not committed to marriage, but because that is their only commitment. Marriage is symbiotic, it lives off of and derives power from our other commitments. When marriage is constricted to a relationship between two people, rather than a practice of the whole church, marriage tends to collapse under its own weight. Marriage alone, the relationship of two detached individuals clinging to one another, isolated from some larger good other than the emotional or economic enhancement of the two individuals, is doomed to collapse. Marriage standing alone, for all its virtues, simply cannot lift the luggage.

18. Hauerwas and Willimon, *Truth about God,* 103.

Therefore, in thinking about marriage we first must think about the church and our vocation to serve Christ, then we move to consideration of how marriage might enhance that vocation. Christians believe that when practiced within the church, marriage liberates us from our own arbitrary desire and gives us something good to do on ordinary days, which are most days, with ordinary people, which means most of us. The sixth commandment thus becomes not some impossible demand, but a gracious invitation to ordinary people to become rather extraordinary saints who are known for their lifetimes of fidelity.[19]

Not only are many churches today seeking new grounding in the "old, old story" and striving to understand its externally-focused place as God's mission in the world, but Christian marriages and Christian families are also in a position of bearing witness and must find new grounding in the same ongoing story of God's faithfulness.

The American culture no longer supports a biblical mandate for the family, if it truly ever did. It is time for an alternative. Over and over again in the biblical story we see examples of those who followed God's direction and knew God intimately enough to risk being counter-cultural—enough to claim their allegiance to a holy nation (see 1 Pet 2:9–10) that is in this world but not *of* it: the Kingdom of God. And in so doing, they influenced the world.

So the question we must ask ourselves is this: Do we know the biblical story well enough to find our identity, purpose, direction, and our place in that community of the faithful? Are we immersed in God's story deeply enough that we can risk being Kingdom-focused and witnesses to an alternative that will replace hyper-individualism with community, consumerism with service and mission, therapy with a discipleship that leads to the freedom of God's Truth, and the busyness and restlessness that

19. Ibid., 103–4.

demand so much of our energy with an ability to be still, and know that God is?

Answering these questions and finding practical solutions for living out marriage and family within a Kingdom of God perspective will be the topic for the rest of this book. My desire is to equip and encourage couples to intentionally live as a model of God's goodness and holiness. My desire is to empower and enable parents to train up their children to see themselves as citizens of an alternative Kingdom and members in God's ongoing story of faith and redemption.

CONVERSATION STARTERS

For engaged couples and newly married couples:

1. Talk about your definition of a "missional attitude" and how you might go about developing that sort of Kingdom-focused attitude as you establish your new life together.

2. Talk about David Thomas' take on the essence of holy matrimony as:

    - a true and enduring participation in God's community

    - a foretaste of heavenly community

    - the essence of effective discipleship, and an enduring witness to an unbelieving world

3. What does this mean to you and your plans for your new family?

4. Hauerwas and Willimon make the statement that: "some marriages today are miserable not because people are not committed to marriage, but because that is their only commitment."

- Discuss and then write down a list of your top 3 commitments as you begin your life together.

For families with children:

1. In what ways does your marriage and family make a Kingdom statement to the world? See if you can think of 3 examples.

2. If missional families seek to be salt, light, and leaven in their communities, and missional parents seek to bring salt, light, and leaven into the ways in which they nurture their children to be worthy citizens of God's Kingdom. What does that really mean and why is it important (or not) for your family?

3. How might you think of yourselves as God's best hope for your community both within the church as well as within our local neighborhoods? Does this change your attitude about your calling and your identity?

For Christian educators, pastors and education committees:

1. In response to a cultural framing of the way to do religion, some Christian leaders are now calling for the church to move back to its biblical mandate to become "salt and light" and become a missional outpost for God's Kingdom; and a call for marriage and the family to go back into its God-ordained, biblical purpose.

   - How might you enable and encourage marriages and families to be formed and functioning within a "citizen of God's Kingdom" perspective in your community?

- How radical would it be in your congregation to suggest that families move beyond the idea of *sending* their children on a youth spring break mission trip to *going together* on intergenerational mission experiences together as a family?

2. Do the families in your church know the biblical story well enough to find their identity, purpose, direction, and meta-narrative in God's Story?

3. Are families in your church community immersed enough in God's Story that they can risk being Kingdom-focused and witness to an alternative lifestyle?

3

Identity

Re-Envisioning Who "I Am"

———•◦•———

In the past several decades Protestant Churches in America have highlighted an individual and personal faith, pointing toward personal devotions, personal evangelism, and personal growth as benchmarks. This way of thinking contributes to the idea that "God is a part of my story."

—Michael Novelli

We must learn to discern the extent to which cultural narratives captivate our moral vision, and determine to engage in the reconstructive work of ordering our language and behavior to the horizon of the biblical narrative.

—Cameron Lee

The way we understand human life depends on what conception we have of the human story. What is the real story of which my life is a part?

—Lesslie Newbigin

Without the Scriptures we're all nearsighted.

—John Calvin

Once there was someone who said such amazing things and did such wonderful things that all the people began to follow him, but they didn't know who he was. So one day they simply had to ask him, and he said . . .

—Sonja Steward and Jerome Berryman

WHO AM I? WHY AM I HERE? WHERE AM I GOING? (REVISITED)

For nearly a decade in the Theology of Culture courses at Wheaton College all freshman were required to read a book called *A Family of Faith: an Introduction to Evangelical Christianity*. And so they were all familiar with the story of a family named the Zoblinskis:

> . . . suddenly Mrs. Zoblinski appeared at the dining room door, hands on her hips. 'Act like Zoblinskis!' she shouted. As quickly as the fracas had begun, the food fight ceased . . . [You see,] Tommy has learned his family's expectations and standards through his parents' modeling and the oral traditions of his ancestors which circulate among family members. The child knows something about the family's reputation, which he is now commanded to uphold, because over a period of years and particularly on special occasions he has met various members of the Zoblinski family—grandparents, aunts and uncles, nieces and nephews, and cousins. Like it or not, he is becoming aware that the Zoblinski heritage includes a Zoblinski way of thinking, acting, and viewing the world. [1]

As Christ-followers we need to learn to think, act and view the world as Christians. This does not happen with once-per-week visits to worship and Sunday school. Little Tommy does not and will not learn his place of belonging within the Zoblinski clan unless he lives daily within his family context, gets to know his extended family, and participates in family life and celebrations.

---

1. Okholm and Phillips, *Family of Faith*, 13.

The Hebrew people, our family ancestors in faith, were instructed over and over again to rehearse their identity, their purpose, and their directions as the people called by God. They were instructed to repeat the *shema* as recorded in Deuteronomy 6:4–9[2] every morning and every evening, so that they would know *to* whom they belong and *with* whom they belong.

In the same way the biblical narrative seeks to overcome our reality and create a new reality. When we practice the discipline of fitting our own life story into God's ongoing story, we begin to feel ourselves to be elements in its structure of universal history.[3]

Former religion editor of *Publishers Weekly* Phyllis Tickle said that "there is a certain scandal to what is happening to Bible publishing over the last 15 years." The problem, as she sees it, is that readers are not being challenged to enter the sacred world of the Bible. "We're saying, 'You stay in the culture and we'll come to you.' How are we going to separate out the culturally transient and trashy from the eternal?"[4]

"If we are to live faithfully the stories of Jesus, *we must know them*," writes Tod Bolsinger in his book *It Takes a Church to Raise a Christian*. He goes on to say that if we are going to discern the way of Jesus,

> we must be able to recognize the path that Jesus has trodden, the traveling habits, and the terrain covered in the story of redemption. We must have the depth of understanding that comes from knowing not only individual verses, but whole sections of the Bible. We must understand the themes, the contradictions, the fabric of faithfulness and failure that make up the history of the people of God. We will never make sense of our struggles, suffering, sin, our salvation, sanctification, and service, if we do not know the story and journey of our mothers

2. The message of the shema is reiterated in several locations in the Pentateuch as well as other places in scripture (see also Exod 12:25–28; Deut 11:1–12).

3. Eric Auerbach, as cited in Stroup, *Promise of Christian Narrative*, 81.

4. *The Week*, April 11, 2008, 45.

and fathers in the faith. A people of the story must know, know deeply, and know by heart the story.[5]

My husband, Dennis, loves to tell stories and to read aloud. When our children were growing up he and I were very intentional and proactive about our plans to indoctrinate our children in faith and family. Part of that intentional plan was to have family reading every evening before bedtime. We would all brush our teeth, put on PJs and cozy up in the living room where Dad would read. We moved from our favorite children's books to the children's classics and from the children's classics to some adult classics. Dennis and I included some of those classics we'd always intended to read and had missed as we were growing up.

This family ritual started when our children were just toddlers and continued longer than any of us expected. The last book I remember reading aloud as a family was *Up From Slavery*, by Booker T. Washington, when our kids were 17 and 15—well into their teen years.

During those teen years a guest came to live at our home for eleven months. Yohana was a Palestinian Christian that our family connected with on a Wheaton College study trip to Jerusalem. Yohana, or Hana as we called him, was in graduate studies at Wheaton and later went on to receive his PhD before returning to teach and become academic dean at Bethlehem Bible College. While Hana lived with us that year he loved our family storytime. He'd hurry home every night from classes or from his studies in the library so he'd not miss the family reading time.

---

5. Bolsinger, *It Takes A Church,* 131. Cf. Barna, *Second Coming of the Church,* 122: "For years we have been exposing Christians to scattered, random bits of biblical knowledge through our church services and Christian education classes. They hear a principle here and read a truth there, then nod their head in approval and feel momentarily satisfied over receiving this new insight into their faith, but within the space of just a few hours that principle or truth is lost in the busyness and complexity of their lives. They could not capture that insight and own it because they have never been given sufficient context and method."

Reading and telling stories together allows our families to "re-member" and reconnect with who we are in Christ's family. It is part of what gives a sense of identity and a narrative for our families' lives. As our guest, Hana also recognized this as a time of connecting and belonging within our household, a tradition that pulled our household together and "re-membered" us.

One of the things our society today takes from us is the simple joy of reading together and allowing ourselves to be formed by our stories and the stories of others. Unless we're intentional, how often do we ever take the time in our busy lives to tell our own stories and the stories of our faith?

We are a people of stories. The original passing down of the biblical narrative came through verbal transmission of the story. Knowing and repeating our stories fits us into a history and a narrative bigger and broader than ourselves.

In our family's nightly reading we always finished with a reading from our family story Bible. We read it over and over again to our children as they grew up, until the pages were falling out of the binding![6] As a result our children began to see themselves as members of the family of God.

Once when our son made a poor choice in behavior and decided not to tell us about it (we found out anyway since parents have a way of doing that) our nightly reading, by coincidence, was the story of Achan in Joshua 7, reading from Walter Wangerin's *Book of God*. After the reading I confronted our son in private in his room to talk with him about his actions, reminding him of the story we just read that evening and of his biblical ancestor Achan and what happened to him when he chose to deceive God. Our son quickly pointed out to me (without missing a beat) that we now live under grace and not under law! But we know that the people of the Old Testament were also living under God's grace

6. Although we used a popular story Bible at that time, I now recommend the following to families and also give to all of our kindergarten families at St. Andrew's each year: Lloyd-Jones. *The Jesus Storybook Bible*. I recommend it because this one tells the "story beneath" (the story of Christ) all the stories in the Bible. For families with older youth I recommend Wangerin, *Book of God*.

and, as well, that the law is a gracious gift that helps us learn to live as Kingdom people. The experience was a good reminder to us both, and a good reason to learn the stories and lessons in both the Old as well as the New Testament!

When our daughter was in middle school, she went through a time of being afraid to go to sleep with the lights off. Remembering the story of God's protection recorded in Psalm 91 gave both of us the assurance of his care for her. Adding to her bedroom wall the suggestive *Watcher in the Night* painting of the guarding angel of Psalm 91 gave her a constant reminder.[7]

In her book, *One Thousand Gifts,* Ann Voskamp relates a time when her son was so angry with his family and with life in general that she was unable to reason or guilt him out of it. She felt the frustration rising in her own stomach as she tried to redirect the situation. And so she made a choice, but it was a choice born out of her—and her son's—identity within God's story. She asked, "Can I tell you a story?"

> I can feel his muscles relax. Since the day I first held him,
> I've told stories to this curl of ear. He and I, stories, this
> is our space.[8]

She told her son the story of his faith-father, Jacob, who wrestled with God and received a blessing. Because she was part of the story, and the story is part of her and her son, she was able to re-envision his emotion within a Kingdom worldview.

Walter Brueggemann reminds us of the value of story to reach us and change us in ways that instruction never has the power to do, when he says, "The deep places in our lives, places of resistance and embrace, are not ultimately reached by instruction. Those places of resistance and embrace are reached only by stories, by images, metaphors and phrases that line out the world differently, apart from fear or hurt."[9]

7. Blackshear, *Watcher in the Night*, 1995.
8. Voskamp, *One Thousand Gifts*, 122–40.
9. Bruggerman, *Finally comes the Poet*, 110.

A BIBLE IN EVERY HAND; GOD'S STORY IN EVERY HEART

Psalm 78 was a reminder not only to the Jewish nation so long ago, but also serves as a reminder to our generation of Christ followers who live in twenty-first century America.

A man named Asaph, David's music director and writer of twelve of our biblical Psalms, spends 72 verses in Psalm 78 retelling the history and the story of the Jewish nation from the time of slavery in Egypt to David's reign. It was told over and over to each generation of the Hebrew people so they would not forget God and make the same mistakes as their ancestors.

Asaph begins this historic psalm with this admonition:

> 1 My people, listen to my teaching.
> Pay attention to what I say.
> 2 I will open my mouth and tell stories.
> I will speak about things that were hidden.
> They happened a long time ago.
> 3 We have heard about them and we know them.
> Our people who lived before us have told us about them.
> 4 We won't hide them from our children.
> We will tell them to those who live after us.
> We will tell them about what the Lord has done that
> is worthy of praise.
> We will talk about his power and the wonderful things
> he has done.

Steve Kang and Gary Perrott comment, "The psalmist, Asaph, was calling the people to make a *trans-generational* commitment (verses 3–4) to remember the stories of faithfulness from their ancestors in the family of God and bind them to the present and future generations so they would know their identity and begin to think like a family member of God's Kingdom."[10] Let's now resume the Psalm:

> 5 He gave laws to the people of Jacob.
> He gave Israel their law.

10. Kang and Perrott, *Teaching the Faith, Forming the Faithful*, 314–15.

He commanded our people who lived before us
to teach God's laws to their children.

Asaph was determined that future generations would not only keep the commands of the Lord (verses 5 and 7b) but that they would also relive the stories of God's faithful deeds to His people. (verses 4b and 7a)[11]

> 6 Then those born later would know his laws.
> Even their children yet to come would know them.
> And they in turn would tell their children.
> 7 Then they would put their trust in God.
> They would not forget what he has done.
> But would obey his commands.
> 8 They would not be like the people who lived before them.
> Those people were stubborn. They refused to obey God.
> Their hearts were not true to God.
> Their spirits were not faithful to him. (NIRV)

Why is Asaph so concerned? One reason is because Israel had forgotten its place in God's story once before, and as a result, had lost sight of its true identity. Judges 2:10–11 tells us that: "After a whole generation had been gathered to their fathers, another generation grew up, who knew neither the Lord nor what He had done for Israel. Then the Israelites did evil in the eyes of the Lord and served other gods." They had failed to pass on the stories and testimonies of their faith and they had failed to cast the vision of that faith to a new generation. The people had lost their connection to a meta-narrative (a larger contextual story) and they were following the lead of the culture around them.

One of the effects of reading, telling, rereading, and re-telling the biblical stories is the powerful way they speak to the human situation even in the midst of the twenty-first century North American context. As I read and reread the stories of Joshua or Judges or Kings I am reminded of the truth of 2 Timothy 3:16–17 (NRSV) that "all scripture is inspired by God and is useful for teaching, for reproof, for correction, and for training in righ-

11. Ibid.

teousness, so that everyone who belongs to God may be proficient, equipped for every good work."

THE STORY AND THE VISION (OR THE STORY OF THE STORY AND THE VISION OF THE VISION)

While in graduate studies at Wheaton College I discovered a truth that has remained with me and shaped much of my view of Christian education, the Scripture, my family life, and my ministry paradigm. This truth came from a hefty volume by Thomas J. Groome titled *Christian Religious Education: Sharing our Story and Vision.*

Groome goes to great lengths to develop the argument that "Christian religious education is a political activity with 'pilgrims in time' that deliberately and intentionally [connects them with] the activity of God in our *present*, to the *Story* of the Christian faith community [down through the history of the church], and to the *Vision of God's Kingdom*, the seeds of which are already among us."[12]

Throughout his book, Groome develops the concept of what he calls shared praxis, defined as a "way of knowing" that unites dialectically both theory and practice, in which each individual Christian's own story and vision (with a small "s" and "v") is integrated with the Christian community's Story and Vision (with capital "S" and "V").[13] In simpler words, it enriches our present-day lives and our daily journey with God to fit our life stories and personal visions into the greater, shared, and ongoing Story and Vision of God's Kingdom.

This concept of fitting into God's ongoing Story and Vision was nothing new to the Hebrew nation and the New Testament church. For them, knowing God was not a speculative exercise or a contemplative removal from the world. Instead, they understood God best by reflectively engaging the world in obedience

12. Groome, *Christian Religious Education*, 25.
13. Ibid., 156.

to God's reign and in response to the experience of God in the midst of history. Groome describes the Incarnation itself as an act of divine praxis—the Word becoming *flesh* in time and place. Eugene Peterson's *The Message* puts this so well in his translation of John 1:14: "the Word became flesh and moved into the neighborhood."

At Wheaton Graduate School I also learned to envision all Christian education as a learning environment in which students were challenged to connect their life experiences to the greater truth of Scripture and vice-versa in what we call "life application."

Making life application was big business in the eighties and nineties in North America. Most conservative curriculum publishers of the 1980s made sure that their products reflected a life application approach to their lessons for children, youth, and adults. So, in my Christian education studies we were infused with visuals such as a ladder: left pole equals "my life experience" while the right pole equals "Truth of God" and the rungs tied the two together into the "life application." The more connections you could make from truth to life and life to truth, the higher you could "climb" in faith. A similar visual is a train track moving up the line with the message: "To really get anywhere in Christian life one must continually lay down track between Truth and Life and travel forward in faith."

As much as I love these visual models for Christian education, I think that in some ways the Christian curriculum publishers and the churches have sold the gospel short. Have we unintentionally communicated that we have our lives (our stories and visions) over here, while God's truth (Story and Vision) is over there, and our job is to take "bits and pieces" of God's truth and make it fit into our twenty-first-century experiences of life? The danger is that we may treat the scripture as a "self-help" manual and misuse scripture in the process. So should it surprise us when studies such as Smith and Denton's *Soul Searching: the Religious and Spiritual Lives of American Teens*[14] show us that

14. Denton and Smith, *Soul Searching*.

those teens who grew up in churches where the "bits and pieces" of God's truth were made to fit into our life experiences now see God as moralistic and therapeutic?

This all came to light for me as I began to read and listened to the message of folks such as Craig Bartholomew and Michael Goheen. Their book *The Drama of Scripture* reminded me that "human communities live out some story that provides a context for understanding the meaning of history and gives shape and direction to their lives. If we allow the Bible to become fragmented, it is in danger of being absorbed into whatever other story is shaping our culture, and it will thus cease to shape our lives as it should."[15]

Over these past twenty years as a Christian Educator have I been guilty of fragmenting the Bible? Have our wonderful and developmentally appropriate curriculum publishers done the same?

Not only that, but have we inadvertently created a *personal* reality in which to live our faith? In trying to make a life application, have I worked too hard to fit God's Kingdom message into my personal faith and personal devotions so that my personal growth becomes my highest goal?

I appreciate the way that Michael Novelli puts it: "In the past several decades Protestant churches in America have highlighted an individual and personal faith which point toward personal devotions, personal evangelism, and personal growth as benchmarks. This way of thinking contributes to the idea that 'God is a part of *my* story.'"[16]

I want God to be part of the story of my marriage and the vision for my family and, of course, a part of my children's story and vision. But even more than that, I want our family to be challenged to be part of God's over-arching and ongoing story in a history and future that is so much bigger than us!

15. Bartholomew & Goheen, *Drama of Scripture*, 12.
16. Novelli, *Shaped by the Story*, 63.

Another inherent danger of life application model in ministry is putting more emphasis on *how* we want our children to live without a deeper connection to *why* they live. Over the last few decades some Christian educators and parents have risked focusing on little more than behavior modification in our children.

> Are we motivating people to live for a story that isn't their own? I fear that most [youth] don't even know why they're supposed to live for God because we've focused so much on how we expect them to live. We've provided only limited views and shallow pictures of the kingdom of God in which we're called to live. We need to stop trying to *fit* God into our lives and stories and realize that God desires us to play a role in his Story instead.[17]

As Dan Kimball states, "We seem to have raised a generation of young people who do not know the Bible and don't have a church background."[18]

As I now understand it twenty years hence, Thomas Groome's concept of shared praxis learning is a foundational look at what it means for us as a Christian community/ family to reorient ourselves and our children from our small "stories and visions" into God's Kingdom. Within community, Groome writes, and in a context of intentional religious education, the educator [parent] has the responsibility of ensuring that the Story is encountered and its Vision proposed.

In the community encounter between our own stories and God's Story, between our own visions and God's Vision, we can come to know God in an experiential and reflective manner. It will be a shared praxis way of knowing that arises from our own praxis, from the praxis of our community of pilgrims in time, and from the praxis of God in history. Groome writes that the Story is the Story of the Kingdom; the Vision is the Vision of the

17. Ibid., 96.
18. Kimball, *Emerging Church*, 44.

Kingdom. The Vision is our response to and God's promise in the Story, and the Story is the unfolding of the Vision.[19]

If our journey in life is to unfold God's Vision rather than merely repeat the past, then the present cannot passively inherit and repeat the Story; it needs to be actively inherited by each generation. And so, thankfully, Groome and others remind us of the need for critical biblical scholarship and theology to inform us as we attempt to critically appropriate the traditions of God's Story and Vision down through history.

"In our present age of the ongoing Christian journey, we are invited to step onto a moving train."[20] (Perhaps a better analogy than that of laying down our own tracks as in the life application model?) In other words, the Story and Vision of God's Kingdom being worked out in this world has been going on long before we came onto the scene. And more than laying down our own tracks and picking and choosing "bits and pieces" for *our* own journey, we need to realize that we're getting onto that moving train with a lot of other passengers, biblical characters and saints down through our church's history, who have traveled longer and seen more sights than we can imagine.

We must dialogue with those other passengers, and nurture our children to dialogue with them, and hear how their stories and visions have fit into the Story and Vision of God's Kingdom purpose.[21]

---

19. Groome, Christian Religious Education, 193.

20. Hauerwas and Willimon, *Resident Aliens*, 52.

21. This is one of the potential dangers in using *only* a "small group" or "koinonia group" model for Christian education, we must be careful that our education does not consist solely of sharing our thoughts and feelings but also stays informed by Biblical scholarship and commentary.

WHERE DOES MISSIONAL FIT
INTO THE STORY AND VISION?

As we grow in our love, as we grow in our Godly calling as a married couple and as a family, as we rehearse our story within God's Story of his people, and as we line up our vision with God's vision for his Kingdom, we are better equipped to be the presence of Christ in the lives of those in our community, our family, and our world.

> Being the presence of Christ in the world moves us toward a missional model for our families. Following this missional model means that we choose to participate in God's mission adventure rather than our own. Approaching a missional mindset means that we engage in a missional journey. The missional model is about empowering one another to use our passions with intentionality to be the presence of Christ to others. This missional model creates a mindset in which we look for ways to participate in the Kingdom of God. Imagine a marriage / a family that is less about consumerism and more about servanthood. Our families could change the world! This missional model provides ways for us to confront ourselves with the presence of Christ and move to more meaningful ministry and more honest relationships.[22]

As we create a missional ethos in our marriage and in our family we begin to see ourselves within the narrative of God's overarching story down through history, and as we rehearse and remember God's Story we really do *re-member* and reorient our lives into a belonging community of the faithful and "we no longer are conformed to this world but begin to be transformed by the renewing or our hearts and our minds" so that the culture can no longer so easily "squeeze us into its mold" (see Rom 12:2, *The Message*).

22. Prosser, Coordinator of Congregational Life for the National Cooperative Baptism Fellowship. bprosser@thefellowship.info.

Using "I Wonder" Questions
to Develop a Kingdom Imagination

Over my years of ministry as well as my years of living married life and raising children within God's Kingdom focus, I have found it useful to use a series of "I wonder" questions at the end of a Bible story to help my children or audience engage and internalize the meaning of the story. So, I wonder if the following lists and models will inspire your family's place in God's story?

For example:

- I wonder how God feels when we come together to worship Him? I wonder if it makes God smile?

- I wonder how big our family really is? I wonder who really belongs to our family?

- I wonder where the "Kingdom of God" might really be?

- I wonder how the disciples felt when Jesus called them to leave their daily routine behind and come and follow him and become part of his kingdom?

- I wonder how Jesus disciples felt when they saw Jesus welcoming the children?

This model of teaching with "wondering questions" comes from "Godly Play" by Jerome Berryman.

CONVERSATION STARTERS

Focusing Outward: Habits to try on . . .

1. Try reading a Bible storybook aloud together as a couple (or as a family) with the purpose of finding your historical Christian family roots. I suggest Walter Wangerin's *The Book of God: The Bible as a Novel* for couples or families with older children; or for couples or families with younger children, *The Jesus Bible Story Book*, by Sally Lloyd-Jones.

2. Talk to your pastor or, better yet, some of the older members of your congregation, and ask them to tell you the stories of your home church family. What makes your community unique and special? Think of venues for sharing these stories within the church family so that youth and children will know their history, their common stories and their place of belonging.

Focusing Inward: Family Bible Talk . . .

1. Read Psalm 78 and/or Hebrews 11 and challenge each other to see how much you can remember about your biblical faith ancestors.

2. Read 1 Peter 1 and 2 and talk about what it means and how it feels to be part of a holy nation and a royal priesthood. Does that influence the way that you function within your usual culture? Why or why not?

4

Direction and Purpose

Re-Envisioning Marriage, Family, Church, and Kingdom

Following this missional model means that we choose to participate in God's mission adventure rather than our own. Approaching a missional mind-set means that we engage in a missional journey.

—Bo Prosser

Jesus called the church to be a family of families. Today the church more often resembles a corporation or a mall of specialty shops than a family.

—Pamala Erwin

We believe in another way of life—the Kingdom of God— which stands in opposition to the principalities, powers and rulers of this dark world (Eph 6:12).

—Shane Claiborne

Day by day, as they spent much time together in the temple, they broke bread at home and ate their food with glad and generous hears, praising God and having the goodwill of all the people. And day by day the Lord added to their number those who were being saved.

Acts 2:46–47 (NRSV)

*If Christianity is what it claims to be, then it should be pro-
ducing a type and order of life which is quite exceptional.
If therefore, we are to meet the challenge of the modern
world we must be living the Christian life; and the question
arises how we are to do so.*

—David Martyn Lloyd-Jones

WHY MARRY? OR WHY GOD CREATED MARRIAGE

WHEN DENNIS AND I met while students at Wheaton
College, he felt a strong calling from God to go into youth
ministry—as a single person. So strong was his calling that falling in love with someone really messed up what he sensed to be
God's purpose for his life. I felt a calling to serve God, too, but
at that time it was more of a calling to actually make it through
college and graduate! At the ripe old ages of 19 and 20 we were
faced with a dilemma: What was it that God expected of us
or had planned for us? We were very clearly in love, and our
backgrounds and interests seemed to complement each other
perfectly.

Dennis still felt pretty sure that God was calling him to remain single in ministry and having to provide time and resources
for a wife and marriage didn't seem to fit. So he prayed, we prayed,
and he also sought wise counsel from his home church pastor.

We prayerfully considered how we could *best* serve God's
Kingdom: individually or as a married couple. After more prayer,
conversation, and ministering to high school kids together, we
both came to the conclusion that God was calling us to use our
marriage for his Kingdom purposes, and our "mission statement"
was formed and has remained our mission now for thirty-eight
years of married life. Our mission statement: *We can serve God's
Kingdom better together than we can apart.* This mission statement has not only formed us over the years, it has reminded us of
who we are and to which narrative our lives belong; it has driven
our decisions and life choices and it has given us the opportu-

nity to work together for a common goal within God's Kingdom vision.

If Christians decide to marry, I firmly believe that if they seek God's purpose in the company of the Christian community, God does not and will not call them to incompatible missions. Contrary to what even the leadership in some churches model in their own marriages, God's calling is not individualized and personal but rather corporate and interdependent.

THE PLANS I HAVE FOR YOU . . .

The prophet Jeremiah, writing to the exiles in Babylon, encouraged them to continue to seek God's plan and purpose in their lives (even while in bondage!), and to pray for the pagan nation that enslaved them. Even in the midst of an unforeseeable future and distressing situation when they surely found it difficult to keep on praying (especially for those in earthly authority over them), Jeremiah reminded them that God was calling them, as a nation—together, not individually—for a purpose.

Jeremiah's famous words (which are often taken out of context) told them that God would come for them and fulfill His gracious promise to bring them back out of captivity. "For I know the plans I have for you," declares the Lord, "plans to prosper you and not to harm you, plans to give you a hope and a future" (Jer 29:11, NIV) A lot of believers stop at verse 11, take Jeremiah's words as a personal, individualized promise just for them, and claim a "prosperity gospel message," believing that God wants nothing more than to make them happy and fill their lives with *perceived* blessing. However, Jeremiah goes on (and here, I believe, is the message for Christ's Kingdom followers today): "'Then you will call on me and come and pray to me, and I will listen to you. You will seek me and find me when you seek me with all your heart. I will be found by you,'" declares the Lord, "'and will bring you back from captivity'" (Jer 29:12–14, NIV). Here is a model for our lives, our marriage, our family, and our community to focus us and show us God's calling for His family:

1. Both call to me *and* pray to me. (vs. 12a)

2. and (then) I will listen. (vs. 12b)

3. Seek me *with all of your heart*. (vs. 13)

4. and (then) I will be found. (vs. 14)

5. and I will gather you from all the nations and bring you back to me. (vs. 15) (note the promise is "to bring you back to me"—not to fulfill all your "felt needs")

"The first man and woman were not created simply to be companions, but to be companions *in the work* (see Genesis 1:26—28). Families have a purpose," writes Diana Garland, "and a calling from God to be on mission together."[1]

Nowhere in Scripture does God say that his plan is to make you happy or to put you in a marriage solely for your happiness and fulfillment. God's plan for marriage is for us to better participate in the Kingdom of God and model Christ's commitment to his Church for a longing world. God's plan, as Gary Thomas reminds us, may be more to make us *holy* than it is to make us *happy*. So, our "Okholm marriage mission statement" is not so unique; it should be the very basic mission of any Christian marriage! The interesting thing is this: in the same way that we find the paradox of true freedom in obedience, we find true happiness in marriage by seeking to be obedient to God's purpose for our lives.

When the world asks why marry, our marriage and family—as a Kingdom mission for Christ and his Church—should be equipped to answer: to bring hope; to partner with God; to serve better in partnership than singleness. Or, as Gary Thomas puts it so well, "God did not create marriage just to give us a pleasant means of repopulating the world and providing a steady societal institution for the benefit of humanity. He planted mar-

---

1. Garland, *Family Ministry*, 374.

riage among humans as yet another signpost pointing to his own eternal spiritual existence."[2]

> It is sad when something so profound as living out an analogy of Christ and his church is reduced to experiencing this relationship as merely something that will help us avoid sexual sin, keep the world populated, and provide a cure for loneliness. . . . If I believe the primary purpose of marriage is to model God's love for his church, I will enter this relationship and maintain it with an entirely new motivation, one hinted at by Paul in his second letter to the Corinthians: "So we make it our goal to please him." What is your goal? Rather than asking, "What will make me happy?" we are told that we must ask, "What will make God happy"?[3]

SACRED ROMANCE

Culturally and historically the primary purpose of marriage has been procreation and raising families. As I wrote in chapter one, throughout history this was usually handled (at least up until the mid twentieth century) within the context of a larger, extended family community.

With the advent of the literature of the Romantic period of the eighteenth century and exacerbated by advertising, movies, and TV in the mid-twentieth century, a new expectation has been placed on marriage: romance and intimacy. Of course God had the original corner on the market of intimacy when in the very beginning of the Bible God told us that a man leaves his father and his mother and is united to his wife and the two will become one flesh (Gen 2:24). How might we align our social and emotional values of romantic love and passion with God's Kingdom purposes for our lives together? Again Thomas is helpful:

> The idea that marriage can survive on romance alone, or that romantic feelings are more important than any other

2. Thomas, *Sacred Marriage,* 24.
3. Ibid., 32.

consideration when choosing a spouse, has wrecked many a marital ship. Romanticism received a major boost by means of the eighteenth century Romantic poets—Wordsworth, Coleridge, and Blake, followed by their successors in literature, Byron, Shelley, and Keats. These poets passionately argued that it was a crime against oneself to marry for any reasons other than "love" (which was defined largely be feeling and emotion), and the lives of many of them were parodies of irresponsibility and tragedy.[4]

Romance and intimacy undergird a healthy marriage and not only strengthen but also serve as a model for the relationship between God and the Hebrew people (in the Old Testament) and Christ and His Church (in the New Testament). From the very beginning of God's story, male and female were seen as beings created in the image and likeness of God and placed within a covenant relationship of marriage.

That is the primordial image of God, and God says, "Be fruitful and multiply. Let the two become one," and they discovered in this act of marriage how the oneness is more than just a fleeting emotion. It's more than just a physical sensation, it becomes a real fact. It becomes a metaphysical reality because when the two become one, nine months later you've got to give that "one" a name, and that child embodies the oneness that the two became—to show those two that God has designed their oneness to be permanent, to be exclusive, to be life-giving and therefore, to be faithful.[5]

So from the very beginning of God's story in the book of Genesis, apart from any statutes and ordinances or do's and don'ts, "God is telling the story of His own family and how He created his family

4. Ibid., 14.

5. Hahn, *Christ and the Church* (excerpted from the transcript of Scott Hahn's audio and video tape presentation, "Christ and the Church: A Model for Marriage" as it appears in the "Catholic Adult Education on Video Program" with Scott and Kimberly Hahn).

to reflect himself because our God, in the Blessed Trinity, is an eternal family."[6]

Romance for the Christian couple should be so much more than the world, the media and the advertisers model for us. That's just one reason why, in our romantic relationship, Dennis and I intentionally resist the "Hallmark ordained" celebrations: we never celebrate Valentine's Day, nor even Mother's Day or Father's Day with each other.[7] Instead we celebrate days such as St. Benedict's Feast Day on July 11 because the writing of Benedict has so impacted our relationship and helped to form the purpose and direction for our life together. Or we celebrate our own special days such as the anniversary of our first date, the first day of spring. I've even been surprised to come downstairs to discover a gift of balloons and theater tickets on the morning of our 4,000th day-aversary! Those celebrations of our relationship are romantic indeed, and actually so much more than the usual ideals of romantic love portrayed in media. (And it is certainly more romantic for me to be surprised and honored that Dennis took the time to figure out our 4,000th day of marriage rather than getting a dozen roses and a card because advertisers have reminded him that it's Valentine's Day and he's expected to do so.)

Intimacy and romance for the Christian marriage should be so much more than the world models for us. What I teach our fifth graders and their parents in our fifth grade Family Milestone, *Preparing for Adolescence: Rites of Passage I,* is that the media does not make *too much* of sex and intimacy—they make *too little* of it! God created sexual intimacy based on a covenantal relationship. We have the enriching opportunity to foster a deep covenant of friendship and partnership with each other and with Jesus Christ together.

6. Ibid.

7. Garland, *Family Ministry,* 375–76. "Rather than [churches] celebrating our culture's Mother's Day or Father's Day—which exclude many—congregations can celebrate Faith-Mother's Day and Faith-Father's Day and Faith-grandparent's day. Congregational members can find ways to recognize those who have mothered and fathered them in the faith."

You may remember lighting a unity candle in your wedding ceremony. It is intended to serve as a visual reminder that our "light" for Christ in this world can shine brighter together than individually. We are called to become one in Christ. However, it is not only within the bonds of matrimony that we become one in Christ. We are called to live and minister in unity with the whole body of Christ (Eph 4). We are then instructed to live in *mutual* submission, not only within our marriage but within the whole body of Christ (Eph 5).

By God's design, it is within that communal calling of unity and submission that our intimacy takes on more depth and meaning and pleasure. Only within the purpose of God's Kingdom can romance and sex and intimacy be contextualized and become the things that God designed them to be. As Scott Hahn reminds us,

> If we make [sexual intimacy] the be-all and end-all, I can tell you for sure, our marriages will flounder. Sexual intimacy is not meant to be fireworks, but rather glowing embers that God uses to bring the warmth of covenant love and life into everyday experience.[8]

Another way in which the secular idealized romantic love works against our call to be missional in kingdom-focused marriage is that "romantic love tends to isolate the couple, marginalizing the traditional third parties to marriage." The extended families, the community, the church, and the state, and perhaps even God himself—are all "reduced to spectators applauding the all-conquering love of the two individuals."[9]

As with many other Kingdom-focused marriages, Dennis and I have discovered over the years of marriage that it is within the community and our mutual commitment to life together in worship, service, education, and fellowship that we have found a deeper purpose and unity. This deeper purpose and unity actually enriches our intimacy and our communication in our alone

8. Hahn, *Christ and the Church*.
9. Ibid.

times. It is by embracing our common calling to participate in the Kingdom of God and God's purpose that we are brought closer and into deeper fellowship with each other. This works against our cultural value of private space and individualism and brings us, instead, into a sacred space and community.

MARRIAGE, FAMILY, AND CHURCH FAMILY: A WITNESS TO CULTURE

The emphasis on individualism within our culture actually takes on a unique character when we see the impact it has on marriages. Although we go through the beautiful rituals of the marriage ceremony, the institution of marriage has been relatively removed from the sacredness of the church to become more of a legal contract. Alan Wisdom writes:

> In the law and political philosophy, thinkers starting with the 18th century Enlightenment conceived marriage as just another kind of contract. Of course, there had been marriage contracts between families for thousands of years. But modern liberalism narrows the parties to just the two individuals being wed. Those two individuals can set the terms of their contract however they please. Each couple defines its own marriage, rather than looking to God or cultural tradition for some external definition. The recent practice of couples writing their own vows reflects this individualist approach to marriage.[10]

If marriage is only seen as a legal contract between individual parties, then if or when it no longer serves the interests of the contracting individuals, the contract is fairly easily dissolved. This has become particularly true since the introduction of no-fault divorce laws in the 1970s.

The law increasingly looks at the spouses in a marriage contract as two autonomous individuals, and more and more this contract is looked at as a temporary partnership. In many cases today, individuals who enter into a marriage contract

10. Wisdom, "Is Marriage Worth Defending?" Part II, 1.

without a written prenuptial agreement are considered naïve at best. "Marriage has become one of the least enforceable contracts under U.S. law."[11] In part this is because the state has little if any interest in how we live out our marriages as long as we don't physically harm each other.

As I discussed in chapter one, it is important to recognize a movement toward individualism in the way we do church in our culture, which directly impacts marriages and families that make up our churches. It might be said that as unity and commitment go in the community of marriage, so goes the unity and commitment in the community of church.

Over the past seven decades in America (beginning in post-World War II America), the institutional church has become increasingly fragmented as a response to or as an accommodation to the culture. This accommodation has partially happened in response to increased leisure time and affluence competing with God for our time and attention. Adding to this was the establishment of an extended and somewhat carefree age of adolescence that came to be referred to as "teenager" by the mid-1940s.

> The concept of an extended and segregated length of adolescence exacerbated fragmentation of the church community. In order to compete with the American culture for the "teenage" mind and heart, the church looked to the culture for the model of how to communicate with this newly formed demographic. This accommodation included youth groups and youth worship and newly designed church school curriculum aimed at linking the biblical view of community with cultural perspectives on teenage values.[12]

The 1940s through the 1970s also gave rise to new studies on how children learn and new theories of human development. The influence of these new studies resulted in an increase of social science-based educational theories being incorporated into the

11. Ibid., 2.
12. Bergler, "I Found My Thrill," 123–49.

way churches educated their youth and children. Complicating all of this were the cultural accommodations for increased technology and sweeping media influence on the church.

In general, during the last half of the twentieth century, we saw a move away from an earlier culture that *supported* the church and family toward one that *competed* with the church and family in all aspects from education to leisure activities. All this combined resulted in a move away from the church's primary task of building strong, vibrant families in *intergenerational community* (as well as the church's mandate to serve a lost and broken world) and backed the church into a position of competing with culture for the minds and hearts of its youth.

Competition with the culture became accommodation to the culture. And as I said above, one of the ways in which the church competed with and accommodated the changes in culture was by developing a programmatic structure that has separated the local church into age-segregated communities within the community, such that "church programs have viewed families as a collection of individuals at different places in the developmental process—children, youth, young adults, middle adults, senior adults."[13] In so doing, the churches of the last half of the twentieth century have inadvertently bought into the cultural value of individualism, which has had ramifications for the church as a whole as well as for the families that make up the church.

Now, however, many church leaders are recognizing the impact of such programmatic divisions. We stand on the precipice of a new dawn in congregational ministry and a new opportunity to bring marriages and families into a Christ-centered community instead of individualized programs. There is a renewed emphasis on doing Family-Centered Ministry, Family-Based Youth Ministry, Family-focused Children's Ministry, all in keeping with a renewed goal of community.[14] You might say that we're moving

13. Garland, *Family Ministry*, 394.

14. Ibid., 12. "This new emphasis on doing "Family Ministry" has been defined as the process of intentionally and persistently realigning a congrega-

from the *dis-integration* of the last part of the twentieth century to the *re-integration* of the twenty-first century. This is good news for families that need to be supported by the church.

The church in North America appears to be consciously rejecting the implementation of a culturally influenced individualistic, programmatic model and beginning to promote a holistic and biblically mandated family unity. In so doing the church is becoming consciously more missional, and one of the purposes of this book is a call to families within the church to get excited about our witness to a world hungering for community.

However, beside the threat of individualism and a hunger for re-integration in our churches, there is that other issue that continues to threaten the foundation of marriages and family in our culture—an insidious threat that keeps the church from being the witness of unity and community that our world so desperately needs. I am referring to the threat of consumption that fosters an overwhelming desire for more: more stuff, more time, more power, more influence, more connections, more sex, more appeal . . . and the list goes on and on. It often dictates the way we present the church's mission and practice community.

MARRIAGE, FAMILY, AND KINGDOM VALUES: A WITNESS TO CULTURE

To consider the greatest threats to our American families, Rodney Clapp notes that "Christian family advocates present a list commonly including pornography, drugs, public schools and secular humanism."[15] However, Clapp suggests that although such factors challenge and can hinder Christian family, there are two things that bother him about that "accepted list of enemies to the family." First he warns that the list "lets Christians off the hook," while "it shoves the real enemies of our family outside our

---

tion's proclamation and practices so that parents are acknowledged, trained, and held accountable as the persons primarily responsible for the discipleship of their children."

15. Clapp, *Families at the Crossroads,* 51.

camp." That list of evils does not go deep enough and fails to ask exactly what it is about our cultural setting and our values that so incline us to eroding families. Why is it that many Christian family advocates fail to look critically at the suburban lifestyle the Christian family often embraces?

> These advocates often fail to consider what may underlie pornography or drug use and the failure of Christian family. The deeper problem? To put it bluntly, the deeper problem is that capitalism has succeeded. Capitalism has given us a more materially prosperous world, fostered creativity and given us a wide array of desirable choices, so any criticism of it demands some nuance.[16]

Just like the culture around us, many North American families have a felt need for stuff and more stuff to keep them happy, to give purpose and meaning in life. The result is momentary meaning and happiness that lasts for a while until it grows too familiar, followed by a search for new stuff to fill the happiness quota. This constant seeking turns out to be not only for stuff but also for *people* to fill our happiness quota. We need new idols to follow, we need new role-models, new and more Facebook friends and Twitter-followers.

"Happiness is like getting a new car," says Jonathan, a successful lawyer who found himself dragged into working in an inner-city mission by his wife, Grace. "It smells new, and you drive it for a while and then it gets dirty, and it's not new anymore. It's nice, but it's not new and the happiness factor starts going down, and then to get back to happy again, you've got to get another new car." Jonathan commented that he had finally discovered something more than happiness, he had discovered joy. How? He found a fulfillment in working with the families at a local inner-city mission that was a lot more meaningful for him and his family "than playing golf on Saturdays like the other lawyers in his firm." "Over time," Diana Garland writes of this story of Jonathan and his wife Grace, "the family's involvement in the

16. Ibid.

mission has become the center of their lives together."[17] Jonathan comments that when he and his family are serving together, the "joy is there even after whatever it is that you're involved in is finished, there's something that resides in you. It makes you smile in the middle of the day and you can't think of anything in particular that's happening. It just clothes you."[18]

We in our North American culture are entering a time of capitalism overload and media saturation. More than we have experienced in the past half century, and perhaps as a result of finding too much stuff unsatisfying, middle class Americans are seeking after something of lasting value. Capitalism may have given us a more materially prosperous world and a wide array of desirable choices, but some families are discovering that service is an antidote to the cultural value of consumerism. Friends, married couples, and family who work together often experience a strengthening of their bond, a new dimension of shared experience.

This situation has been exacerbated by the fact that most suburban and urban families in our culture no longer have a need or means of *producing* anything together and their sole relational function is based on what they *consume* together. So their conversations and their actions are reduced to planning for the next purchase, next vacation, next entertainment event, rather than actually working toward an accomplishment or project. This is why the current missional vision within our church communities is so important for couples and families. Yet too often mission and service are seen as individualized projects within a community, apart from one's nuclear family—an age-segregated activity such as a youth mission trip.

There is this encouraging movement toward service and giving back in communities today. Even an official program called Serve Day has become a national movement and a catalyst to getting individuals and families involved in serving their

17. Garland, *Inside-Out Families*, 57–58.
18. Ibid.

communities.[19] Churches have joined this Serve Day movement as a means of becoming more externally-focused and missional. Disneyland has jumped on the bandwagon with their Give a Day, Get a Day program for encouraging families to serve together (albeit for the reward of a free day at Disneyland!). Still, it was a sad comment on our culture when our church's participation in the Serve Day program was one of the few intergenerational offerings on the Disney website in which parents could participate with their children.

Diana Garland writes about her research on families that serve together in her new book *Inside-Out Families*. In the Families in Faith project she used grant money to conduct whole-congregation surveys focusing on more than one hundred Protestant congregations throughout the U.S., and over the past fifteen years. This study identified the powerful role of family stories and families serving together. In the conclusion of this study she writes that the heart of the church's call to minister to families "is equipping families together for a life of Christian service to others beyond themselves, to turn themselves inside out in a calling larger than their own daily life together. As they serve others, they grip a deeper understanding of one another and of God. They find their faith more resilient and meaningful."[20] They also find a means of producing something rewarding and worthwhile together over against the more common function of solely consuming together, and in so doing they are strengthening their relationships with one another and becoming more of what God intended.

Garland and her team coined the phrase "sticky faith" to define the outcome of generations serving together in community who develop a sticky faith that keeps them stuck to the church and to God, and carries them through the crises and deep struggles that life inevitably holds. When our Christian marriage and

---

19. www.serveday.org.

20. Garland, *Inside-Out Families*, 11.

family models the value of service and Kingdom purpose, they become a witness against the consumer culture.

When our churches become more concerned with our ministry *through* families instead of promoting our ministry *to* families and stop trying to market the services of the church to make you "healthier and happier" then we, altogether, will be in a better position to develop a "sticky faith."

WE BELIEVE IN ANOTHER WAY OF LIFE: COUNTERING MORALISTIC THERAPEUTIC DEISM

In the online magazine *Relevant*, Shane Claiborne explains "why easy living isn't necessarily better living." He says that from his experiences in life he began to wonder what it might look like if people who call themselves followers of Christ really decided to follow Jesus.

He wondered what a fully devoted Christian might look like. He writes that he "knew we were not going to win the masses to Christianity until we began to live it. So I went looking for a Christian, hoping to find someone else who might be asking, *What if Jesus meant the stuff He said?*"[21]

In his letter to the new believers in the city of Ephesus, Paul wrote that we wrestle against the powers and principalities of this world, and in order to take a stand for God's Kingdom we must live our lives a different way, or as Paul put it, we must "put on the armor of God" (Eph 6) In our Kingdom-focus for marriage and family, we must believe in another way of life that goes against the present values of our culture. We must practice daily the presence of the Kingdom of God, which stands in opposition to the principalities, powers, and rulers of this world.

Belonging to and finding identity in a bigger story and focusing on a deeper vision for God's acts in human history (as talked about in chapter three of this book) moves us away from seeking a *personal* God to fulfill all our felt needs and desires in

21. Claiborne, *Irresistible Revolution*, 72.

a moralistic, therapeutic way. It moves us toward a way of recognizing and naming God's purpose and direction for our lives within a life-forming community of faith. And, as Tod Bolsinger puts it so well, this *is* mission: "The call of Jesus to be the savior of the world, leads to his people being a community of witness to that saving love in the world. In short, our community is not only *for* witness, it *is* witness."[22] And as the early church modeled, day by day, the new believers spent time together in a community of worship, they broke bread at home and ate their food with glad and generous hearts, they practiced the praise of God in all things and practiced service and care of all the people. "And the Lord added to their number daily those who were being saved" (Acts 2:47 NIV).

COUNTERING BUSYNESS AND RESTLESSNESS: A WITNESS TO A HIGHER CALLING IN LIFE

Another of Garland's stories in her study of families that had discovered the value of living life and faith from the "inside-out" involves a woman named Heather. Heather commented that she had been restless for a long time, worried and dissatisfied with the role of faith in her family's life which she described as "seemingly just another of the many activity programs that engaged my family's 'spare' time." Heather wanted something more substantial for her family. She desired their faith to be real and central in their lives. By the end of a summer in which Heather made a conscious choice to "drag her family to participate in inner-city ministry, her family who had just spent two hours one weeknight per week (which eventually grew to also include some Saturday mornings playing with kids at the ministry) reported that the experience had changed their understanding of their church, their community, their family, even their faith."

Heather commented that although she set out with the idea of just doing this great thing for these poor kids in the inner-city,

22. Bolsinger, *It Takes a Church*, 139.

she soon came to realize, "My kids need this. They need to have friends like this, who aren't all white and middle class and just like them."[23]

Living marriage and life in family with clear focus and deeper vision of what life can be is virtuous for families (as well as for congregations). It is a cure for busyness by keeping our priorities in line with God's priorities; it is a cure for restlessness by keeping our vision set on God's reality. It is allowing our hearts to be directed (and even broken) by what breaks the heart of God.

CONVERSATION STARTERS

Focusing Outward: Habits to try on . . .

1. How do you react to these statements?

   - "The church is 'first family.'"

   - "The nuclear family is not God's most important earthly institution."

   - "The church does not exist to serve the family; the family exists to serve the church."

2. What do think Jesus meant when he said: "Whoever comes to me and does not hate father and mother, wife and children, brothers and sisters, yes, and even life itself, cannot be my disciple?" (Luke 14:26, NRSV)

---

23. Garland, *Inside-Out Families*, 57.

Focusing Inward: Family Bible Talk . . .

Look at the stories of these three Biblical families and talk about their story and how their life experiences bring purpose and direction to our Kingdom calling in our culture of the twenty-first century:

1. Exodus—the stories of Moses and his family:

   - How did his parents show Godly wisdom? How did the community support and protect their decisions (Exod 2)?

   - What strength did his sister, Miriam, bring to the family dynamics (Exod 2 and Exod 15–20)?

   - What wise advice did he receive from his father-in-law, Jethro, and how did the community come alongside them to fulfill God's purpose (Exod 18:13–26)?

2. Ruth—the story of Ruth and her family:

   - What poor decisions did Ruth's parents-in-law make in disobeying God and moving to Moab? How did God work in their lives in spite of their poor family choices (Ruth 1)?

   - How did Boaz involve and honor the community in making wise decisions (Ruth 3)?

3. Acts—the story of married couple, Aquila and Priscilla:

   - This married couple partnered in business and ministry with Paul. In what ways did they extend their marriage and create a missional focus to further the kingdom of God (Acts 18 and Rom 16:3)?

5

Learning to "See" Better

Re-Envisioning our Habits and Disciplines

What we are teaches our children far more than what we say, so we must be what we want our children to become.

—Joseph Chilton Pearce

We can only act within the world we can envision, and we can envision the world rightly only as we are trained to see.

—Stanley Hauerwas

I wear my lenses, and I pray to see. Who knows when you might climb a mount of transfiguration?

—Ann Voskamp

My eyes account for less than one percent of the weight of my head; I'm bony and dense; I see what I expect.

—Annie Dillard

My father didn't tell me how to live; he lived, and let me watch him do it.

—Clarence Budington Kelland

Launch into the deep and you shall see.

—Jacques Ellul

Learning to "See" Better

When a person looks at me, he sees the one who sent me.
I have come into the world as a light, so that no one who
believes in me should stay in darkness.

John 12:45–46 (TNIV)

A "LENS" TO SEE BETTER: A KINGDOM WORLDVIEW

A WHILE BACK DENNIS and I went to see the movie *Avatar* in 3D. It was beautiful cinematography and an engaging story, perhaps leaning a bit too far toward New Age religion for the comfort of some folks. But as I watched it and especially thought about it on the drive home, it brought to my mind the idea that we are called to become humans who are so deeply connected with each other and with our faith community that we can really learn to *see* the world in a different way than most folks. In *Avatar*, the residents of the planet Pandora greeted one another by saying, "I see you," meaning *I connect with you, I identify with and understand you.* Humans in this movie are portrayed as disconnected, lacking insight, self-serving, acquirers—get what you need no matter what the means or whom you have to destroy along the way. Humans are portrayed as beings that value independence, individual rights, and consumerism more highly than they value community and mutual interdependence.

The people of Pandora were the heroes in this film, not because they were more powerful, but because of their great connectional worldview, a worldview that tells them: *we belong to each other and we're all connected to the earth, our ancestors, other living species.* "I see you" equals "I can look deeply into your soul." Even the horses and flying creatures were connected. There was also a way provided for the people belonging to Pandora to come to their deity in prayer by becoming literally connected.

Being connected to something larger than self and immediate culture, as well as finding our place of *being* within a larger biblical meta-narrative through which we view ourselves and our cultural context, allows us and our children to understand who

we are, why we are here and where we might be going as participants in a larger community of faithful people.

The privilege of Christian parents is to pass on to another
generation the stories of the faithful ancestors in the narrative of
faith (see Ps 78; also Jos 2:10–11, discussed in chapter 3 of this
book) and to give our children spiritual eyes to see. Both John
Calvin and John Wesley write about seeing our world through
the *lens* of Scripture and being trained to see our world in that
frame of reference.

Parents who are connected to a faith community have the
responsibility to train children (through teaching, example, life
together, practice, service together) to see reality in a way that is
defined by the community's vision. Consider this question: Have
we as North American Christians been better at training our
children to see themselves as good Americans than as citizens of
God's Kingdom?

LAUNCHING INTO THE DEEP

Do we really want to see our lives and our world through the
lens of a Kingdom worldview? Are we willing to train and nurture ourselves, as well as our children, to develop *eyes of the soul*
through habits and disciplines that will give real sight into our
purpose as participants in God's Kingdom? It really is not all that
difficult; we simply need to begin to practice seeing our daily
lives through a Kingdom lens. Or, as Ann Voskamp reminds the
readers in her book *One Thousand Gifts,* we don't have to change
what we see, only the *way* we see.[1] "I wear the lens of the word
and all the world transfigures into the beauty of Christ and everything is *eucharisteo.*"[2]

---

1. Voskamp, *One Thousand Gifts,* 135.

2. Ibid., 101. *Eucharisteo* is the Greek word meaning "to give thanks." The
root word is *charis,* meaning "grace" and *charo,* meaning "joy." From this word
we also get one of the common words for communion or the Lord's Supper:
"eucharist."

Eight Practical Ways to Develop a Biblical Worldview

Everyone has a worldview whether they've thought about it or not. It is the way that we see and understand the world around us. *(For one example: it is difficult for those of us raised with a North American cultural worldview to see and understand the "face-saving" and "shame-based" mindset of many Arab and Asian cultures.)*

Although everyone has a worldview, according to a survey by the Barna Research Group, only 4% of American adults have a *biblical* worldview.

Practicing spiritual habits in daily routine begins to correct your biblical "lens" and helps to create a biblical worldview.

1. Read (and study) the Bible: commit to a Bible study group that requires homework.

2. Seek prayer, practice prayer and pray with others regularly.

3. Seek out a spiritual mentor and/or accountability partner or group.

4. Begin to identify yourself and your family within the church year calendar in addition to national calendar so that you begin to be defined by the historical celebrations of your Christian ancestors in faith.

5. Surround yourself and your family with reminders of your faith commitment (such as sticky notes on bathroom mirror and dashboard of your car).

6. Turn off the TV and radio more (especially "talk radio" that quickly forms a different worldview in listeners).

7. Practice the discipline of patience as a means of "widening your capacity" in order to see life differently.

8. Count your blessings each day and practice giving thanks together.

At the beginning of this chapter I cited verses from the Gospel of John. In that passage Jesus had only recently ridden into Jerusalem on a donkey (John 12:12–15). The people were expecting to see an earthly king who would overthrow the Roman rule at the time. They still did not understand. Now Jesus was talking to the crowd that had followed him, trying to help them understand his true mission (vv. 23–36). He told them that "the light" would be with them just a little while longer and then it would be taken away (vs. 35). He encouraged them to become sons and daughters of "the light," (vs. 36) and after he'd finished speaking, the scriptures tell us that "he hid himself." John quotes verses from the prophet Isaiah, saying, "He has blinded their eyes and hardened their hearts, so they can neither see with their eyes, nor understand with their hearts, nor turn—and I would heal them" (vs. 40; also Isa 6:10).

Then Jesus cries out, "'The one who looks at me, is *seeing* the one who sent me. I have come into the world as a light, so that no one who believes in me should stay in darkness" (John 12:45–46 NIV). What's the point? The people in Jerusalem at this time in God's story, just as those in the time of Isaiah, would not believe despite the evidence (see John 12:37). As a result, God hardened their hearts. Does that mean that God intentionally prevented these people from believing in him? No. God simply confirmed their own choices—even after all the miracles, the parables, the history of God's plan and provision in their lives down through the biblical story. They had become so blinded by their cultural worldview that they wouldn't even try to understand Jesus' purpose. So Jesus cries out, "Look at me! Really see me and see God! Believe in me and don't stay in the darkness."

"FOR ONCE YOU WERE IN DARKNESS . . .

. . . but now you are the light of the Lord. Live as children of the light. Wake up sleeper, rise from the dead, and Christ will shine on you" (Eph 5:8, 14–15 NIV).

A way of seeing God's vision more clearly in and for your marriage and your family is to intentionally work on spiritual habits and disciplines. The word "discipline" has such negative and harsh connotations in our culture. With our ethos of self-interest, consumerism, therapy, and busyness, the idea of being disciplined by someone (or disciplining ourselves) is not comfortable.

When I speak to parents about disciplining their children we begin with the etymology of the word *discipline*. It is, of course, related to the word *disciple*. In other words, a parent *disciples* a child, not by punishing but by nurturing and directing. Eugene Peterson writes about spiritual disciplines as a long obedience in the same direction.[3] That is very powerful and convicting imagery: a long obedience goes against our cultural ethos. In our do-it-now and instant-gratification culture, the idea of a long obedience, especially one in the same direction, seems tedious at best. But if I can remind myself that developing spiritual habits and disciplines allows me to become a *seeing* disciple in God's Kingdom, then perhaps I can stay in training and make the extra, un-cultural effort to keep my children in training also.

The verb "to train" as used in the Old Testament book of Proverbs (22:6) is used only four times elsewhere in the Old Testament (twice in Deut 20:5 and once each in 1 Kgs 8:63 and 2 Chr 7:5). In those passages it either means to *dedicate* a newly built family (through marriage) or to *inaugurate* the Lord's temple with sacrifices, as Solomon did. In a similar manner, then, "to train a child" should be construed as initiating or introducing and dedicating the child to the path or journey of the Lord.[4] In other words, beginning a long obedience in the same direction.

Just as the book of Proverbs reminds us to *train* up our children, it also reminds us that "to spare the rod is to hate your child, but the parent who loves the child is careful to discipline him." I appreciate this because the same Hebrew word used in

---

3. Peterson, *Long Obedience in the Same Direction.*
4. Harris, Archer, et al., *Theological Wordbook of the Old Testament*, 301.

Proverbs is also used in Psalm 23:4 to remind us that it is God's *rod* and staff that comfort and direct us to safe pasture, and the same word used Proverbs 29:15 that tells us that the *rod* imparts wisdom.

The point is this: as much as we all dislike the idea of habitual discipline for ourselves as well as for our children, it is the gift of true *sight* that takes us beyond ourselves into God's fulfilling purpose for our lives and for our world.

THE TYRANNY OF THE URGENT

Are you a human *being* or a human *doing*? Often the things that really do matter most are at the mercy of the things that matter least. We all know this to be true, but still the *flesh is weak;* it is so much easier, even in our most important task of being a spouse and raising our children, to succumb to the "quadrant of waste" as defined in Steven Covey's *Time Management Matrix.*[5] By this Covey means that the "important but not urgent" portions of my life are the easiest to neglect. While the "urgent" demands my time and attention, the "not urgent" and "not important" quadrant of the matrix consumes an inordinate portion of my time and attention. Much of this is, of course, an outgrowth of the cultural ethos of individualistic, consumer-driven restlessness that I wrote about in chapter one. However, part of it is simply our human (sinful) nature. Even Jesus' parable of the great feast (Luke 14) addresses our inability to put first things first. The people in the parable all made excuses. C. S. Lewis makes the point in *Screwtape Letters* that the devil captures many not by preventing their spiritual encounters with God, but by whispering at precisely the right moment that just now they are too busy. Another time perhaps?[6] How relevant is the saying: "If the devil can't make you bad, he makes you busy."

5. Covey, *Seven Habits of Highly Effective People.*
6. Lewis, *Screwtape Letters.*

We had a missionary in residence from the Congo who joined our staff and ministry in our church in Glen Ellyn, Illinois a decade ago. He told stories of the serious and pervasive impact of witchcraft in his nation and how there was so much evidence of the work of the evil one in the power that the witch doctors and satanic practices held over his people.

Someone asked him the question of why that was so when, in America, we rarely hear of such things. Why does Satan not demonstrate such demonic power that we can see in our culture? Our Congolese friend responded that perhaps Satan works on us in the areas of our lives that are most susceptible to Satan's influence. In other words, he suggested that Satan may get more results from keeping us too busy for the important work of developing relationships and deeper spiritual lives.

Whereas our scientific mindset can easily explain away the activities of satanic practices such as demons and witchcraft, we can hardly see the negative effects of "the tyranny of the urgent" on our lives, our marriages, and our families.

SEEING YOUR WAY CLEARLY: THE LIGHT AND LENS OF SPIRITUAL DISCIPLINES

Through the years I have observed the outward lifestyle of families in my churches who make a habit of praying together. And when asked, some have told me that praying is a key to their commitment and strength as a family. Most often family prayer takes place at family meals. So if families don't eat together regularly, they don't pray together either.[7]

Making the act of community prayer a habit for your marriage and your family has the power to do so much more than make requests of God. Prayer is a means to equip your family to see better and to bring your family more in line with the acts of the Holy Spirit, to give your family a means of developing a biblical worldview. Prayer unites, gives the means to deeper communication and is a key to commitment and strength.

7. Garland, *Sacred Stories of Ordinary Families*, 72.

Prayer can take on many forms. With just a couple, prayer might be a list of blessings, praise and thanksgiving ending in supplications or *ask-its*. Keeping a list and reflecting on it from time to time is a means of seeing God's faithfulness in your marriage. With young children prayer might be reading a children's book of prayer. It might also be a means to *re-member* who we are and where we belong (prayers for grandparents, faith-family, and others connect children to that bigger story). With older children, prayer can be a means of commitment and accountability.

Writing a prayer or a blessing on a lunch sack or napkin or putting it on a sticky note inside a notebook or school text of an older elementary-aged child can not only strengthen a resolve and a purpose, it can also bring peace and relatedness. Reminding our children that they are connected to God and his Kingdom through the power of prayer or a blessing throughout their daily activities is one of the most meaningful ways of helping them to see better.

Prayer is also a non-threatening way of communicating values and can even become a testimony. I remember when our son was seriously dating a young woman who did not share faith in God but did function within a strong sense of spirituality. After an extended visit in our home and before the kids headed out, I circled the whole family together and said, "Let me ask God's blessings on all of you before you leave." She responded, "Well, I don't know what that means, but I'm up for it." We grabbed hands and I offered up a prayer.

As the saying goes, "prayer changes things." I believe that prayer not only invokes God's presence and God's actions in our world, prayer also changes us. Regular, communal prayer within family is a discipline that begins to change and form us into a Kingdom family.

It is worth noting that habits and disciplines that form us into more Christ-like image are a means and not an end in themselves. Just as prayer not only connects us to the power and presence of God, the practice of regular prayer aligns us to God's will. Prayer and other disciplines are a journey and not the destination. They are a way of adjusting our minds, changing our worldview, shaping our character and conforming our actions after the pattern of Jesus' life. They identify us more firmly with God's Kingdom purposes and help us to work for God's Kingdom "on earth as it is in heaven."

The habits and disciplines that we allow to form our marriage and family life shape the lens through which we see our world as God sees the world.

In Eugene Peterson's *The Message* translation of Paul's letter to the Christ-followers living in Colossae, he writes:

> This mystery has been kept in the dark for a long time, but now it's out in the open. God wanted everyone, not just Jews, to know this rich and glorious secret inside and out, regardless of their background, regardless of their religious standing. The mystery in a nutshell is just this: Christ is in you, so therefore you can look forward to sharing in God's glory. It's that simple. That is the substance of our Message. We preach Christ, warning people not to add to the Message. We teach in a spirit of profound common sense so that we can bring each person to maturity. To be mature is to be basic. Christ! No more, no less. That's what I'm working so hard at day after day, year after year, doing my best with the energy God so generously gives me. (Col 1:26–28, *The Message*)

This then is the message and the mystery in a nutshell: Christ is in you; therefore you look forward to sharing in God's glory. It's that simple. We preach Christ by the way we live each day and we choose for ourselves and for our children to see or not to see the world through the eyes of the Christ revealed in Scripture.

You choose: do you allow your family to be formed by a North American cultural worldview or do you intentionally allow your family to be formed by the spiritual habits and disciplines that might help you to see your way more clearly?

Seven Creative Ways to Pray with Children

1. Give a blessing to your children as they go out into the world each day (before they leave the front door or step out of the car)—a hand placed on a shoulder or head and a brief "Remember, God is with you always," or "May God keep you and direct your journey through this day."

2. Practice a "right ordering" of our prayers and our priorities by training your children to follow the model Jesus taught: begin with praise and adoration, prayers for others, and finally prayers for self. This is simple for young children if you use either:

   — The "Hand Prayer"

   - thumb reminds us to remember God (who created us in his image)

   - index finger reminds us to pray for teachers/parents who instruct us

   - middle finger is the tallest and reminds us to pray for those in authority over us such as principal, police and president;

   - ring finger is our weakest and reminds us to pray for those in need of help and healing

   - little finger is the smallest (but also important) and reminds us to pray for ourselves

   — The "J-O-Y prayer"

   - Jesus (thanks and praise first)

   - Others (thanks and prayers for others in our lives)

   - You ("ask-its" last)

3. Try using a "Bidding Prayer" around the dinner table or at bedtime; saying, "Lord, we pray for . . ." or "Lord, we thank

you for . . ." or "Lord, please forgive us when . . ." and allowing your child to complete the sentence.

4. For older children, use the newspaper, evening news or
Internet to remind us to pray for all people and nations
(broadening their worldview) so that they begin to know
that God is a God of all people and all nations and does not
exist just to serve my needs.

5. Help your child write out a prayer in permanent
marker on the doorpost of your home (or of their
bedroom); on the bed-frame (under the mattress!); on
the inside of the bedroom door as a reminder of God's
presence and purpose for your child's life and for your
family life.

6. Make a flip card on a metal key ring that you can hang
in your car so that you can turn off the music or the
DVD player and talk about faith and life and remember
God's presence in every day life. On the cards, list
things for which your family is thankful. Perhaps also
add some key Bible verses to read aloud together.

7. Practice saying, "let's talk to God about that" when you
find yourself angry, sad, frustrated, anxious, worried,
impatient—and "let's thank God for that" when you
find yourself joyful and blessed.

CONVERSATION STARTERS

Focusing Outward: Habits to try on . . .

1. There are some wonderful book studies on spiritual disciplines, based on the Rule of St. Benedict (see introduction) which my husband and I have found very encouraging as ways to gain better vision for our marriage and our lives as God's Kingdom participants. Among my favorites for couples and families are:

    *   *Spirituality for Everyday Living* by an Episcopal priest, Brian Taylor (only 70 pages long and easy to read with discussion questions at the end of each chapter.)

    *   *The Family Cloister: Benedictine Wisdom for the Home* by a Presbyterian minister, David Robinson. (An easy-to-use guide for parents with lots of practical ideas for developing a Kingdom worldview in your family.)

2. If someone did an inventory of your bank statement and your calendar, how would she describe your life? What might she determine are your habits and priorities? Better yet, do your own inventory of your bank statement and your calendar and decide for yourself what demands your attention and forms your view of the world.

Focusing Inward: Family Bible Talk . . .

1. Read John 12:45 (quoted at beginning of this chapter): we often wonder what God is like since we cannot actually *see* God. Jesus said it plainly, that anyone who sees Him (Jesus) sees God. As we grow up in Christ-likeness in what way do the

habits and disciplines we intentionally incorporate into our daily lives allow other people to *see* God? How do they also help us to recognize or see God better in our marriage and family life on a day in/ day out basis?

2. In Matthew 5:14–16, why does Jesus reminds us to "let our light shine before all people?"

    •   What habits and disciplines do you practice as a couple/as a family that shine a light to help other people see Jesus?

    •   What habits do you practice that might block others from seeing Christ's light? Do you want to change those, really? Why or why not?

6

Freedom in Obedience

Re-Envisioning Our Response-ability

———◆———

Faith is a verb. Faith is a way of behaving which involves knowing, being, and willing. The content of faith is best described in terms of our worldview and value system, but faith itself is something we do. Faith is an action. It results from our actions with others, it changes and expands through our actions with others, and it expresses itself daily in our actions with others.

—John Westerhoff

Those who obey His commands live in Christ, and he in them. This is how we know that he lives in us: by the Spirit he gave us.

1 John 3:24

THE STRENGTH OF OBEDIENCE

AT TIMES JESUS WAS accused, even by his closest disciples, of being too weak and not asserting his power and authority. On one occasion, people couldn't understand why he came riding into Jerusalem on that Palm Sunday if it was not to take over the ruling government and set up an earthly Kingdom. Even his closest disciples did not understand. Jesus did not demonstrate strength and power in the way folks expected.

Using the following object lesson, I have tried to help children (and adults in our congregation) think about what it means to have strength and power that is different from the way our culture often defines these qualities. I show the children a stick and a long blade of grass from my yard and say to them:

> These are both growing things, right? In some ways they're alike; however, in other ways they're very different.
>
> Which one, do you think, is the strongest of these two?
>
> I imagine most people would say the stick, but why?
>
> Why do we immediately believe that a stick is stronger than a blade of grass? Yes, in one way the stick is stronger because you can poke someone or hit something better with it than with the blade of grass; you might say the stick is stronger.
>
> But does strong only mean being able to hit or poke? What about people? When God created strong people did he expect them to show their strength only by hitting or pushing other people around?
>
> The grass doesn't look like it's as strong as the stick, does it? But there is a way that the grass can be stronger than the stick.
>
> Imagine if I try to bend the stick. What happens? It breaks. But I can bend the grass easily.
>
> The stick and the grass have different kinds of strength. Now I have a broken stick. You know why? It's because it breaks in two before it can bend. But let's try this: let's use the strength of the grass to help fix the brokenness of the stick.
>
> The strength of the grass is its ability to bend. I can even wrap it around the broken stick and tie it together to bind the stick and make it straight again. That's something the stick could never do! The strength of the grass is its ability to flex and adapt.[1]

1. Fannin, *Strength in Meekness*, 98.

In one of the sermons he preached, Jesus said the meek are blessed for they shall inherit the earth (Matt 5:5). Rather than thinking of *meek* as *weak,* perhaps it is better to hold to a more biblical concept of being flexible and adaptable. Maybe Jesus knew that some of the people that we call meek or weak are really strong in a different way—like the blade of grass. Maybe meek people are the very ones who are strong enough to help fix the brokenness in God's creation.[2]

Perhaps meekness can bind and bring things and people together. Sometimes Jesus *was* meek because he exhibited a different kind of strength, a quiet strength that people in our world seldom see. Perhaps meekness is just the sort of strength that needs to be developed in order to live well in family, marriage and community relationships. Perhaps we need to cultivate and appreciate a strength that can bend when it needs to and bind together the broken places in our lives. In Ephesians 5, Paul calls us to submit to one another. We are to submit to one another as Christ submitted to the cross. I often think of submitting not as being weak or subservient but as being strong enough in my own identity and purpose to be flexible and adaptable.

Perhaps we need examples of people in our world who are strong enough to be meek, confident enough to be servants, wise enough to be submissive. This turns upside down the values of our culture and allows us to be free, to be who God needs and desires for us to be in our world.

As we submit to Christ and to one another and model that for our families, we begin to get a sense of the Kingdom of God in our lives. Being family is *not* about power plays and levels of authority. We are called to share, support, and encourage, often sacrificially, as Jesus modeled, so that we might truly know abundant life (Eph 5:21–33).

Being in marriage is not about being in a relationship of dependence or a relationship grounded in independence. Why is it that we so often think that those are our only choices? Rather,

2. Ibid.

being in a marriage relationship is about being participants in a relationship of *inter*dependence. Note that I am not talking about a relationship of codependency (at least not the way that it has come to be defined in psychotherapy).[3]

As we make ourselves vulnerable in relationship, we begin to follow God's model for marriage and for family. As we share in the fullness of the family relationship, we understand the true meanings of loving, of being loved and of sharing love. And we begin to understand the call to be involved in God's mission of reconciling the world back to himself, as well as the call to be involved in reconciliation with each other, a call to be more concerned with community than with individual rights and entitlement.

Marital or family relationships that are grounded in God can move us from selfish individualism to a selfless and sacrificial love. As we learn to love and value our true selves, we learn to love and value others. As our identity and purpose are established and reside in something more substantive than individual rights or consumption, we become strong enough to become meek as Christ modeled.

Strong marriage relationships actually lead to more secure individuals. Strong marriages lead to more secure families. Strong families allow us to be vulnerable with one another. Strong relationships put us in a position to receive blessing from God. And we begin to understand that it is in this Christ-like meekness (which I define as interdependence) that our faith sys-

---

3. Garland, *Family Ministry*, 142. A comment is needed here about the current fascination with the phenomenon of "codependency." This term was originally used to describe the coping strategies of family members involving a person with addiction to alcohol, drugs, or other addictive materials. Unfortunately, codependency became a catchy label for *anyone* who met the needs of another person in relationship with the consequence that some have confused attachment and care-giving with family dysfunction. Attachments and care-giving are healthy foundations for family life; they are not signs of family pathology.

tems develop and strengthen and help us to become intentionally focused on and productive in the Kingdom of God.

In chapter eight of John's Gospel, Jesus reveals the key to true freedom. Jesus says that *if* we obey or abide in his teachings, *then* we will be his disciples and we will begin to understand true freedom. Later in chapter 10 John quotes the words of Jesus referring to himself as the good shepherd, in which Jesus says that no one takes his life from him; he lays it down of his own accord.

In the letter of 1 John we again find this message of obedience, of submission and freedom, when John writes that those who obey God's commands live in Christ, and Christ lives in them. And this is how we know that he lives in us: we know it by the Spirit he gave us (1 John 3:24).

These messages of obedience, submission, and abiding in true freedom and understanding are common themes in the writing of John as well as in the letters of the apostle Paul. Paul even writes about putting off the "old nature" and putting on the "new nature" as a means of being freed from bondage to sin. What sort of witness would this lifestyle of freedom be if our marriage and family relationships were so identified in Christ that we practiced true obedience, true meekness, and true submission as modeled by Christ?

MOVING FROM THE CULTURAL VALUE OF INDEPENDENCE TO THE KINGDOM VALUE OF INTERDEPENDENCE

We practice obedience in marriage and family as we seek to be more intentionally aware that we are not in competition with one another—even as our culture often fosters a sense of competition with slogans like: "What's in it for me?"; "Be all that you can be"; "You only go around once in life"; and "Only the best will do."

As our marriage relationship moves intentionally and proactively into a Kingdom focus, keeping up with the "Joneses" should no longer be a driving force. As we move into a Kingdom-focused journey, we need to work toward an understanding that competition never leads to fulfillment. The consumer-driven need to have more in order to feel good about ourselves disappears as we commit to the Kingdom journey together as a married couple or as a family.

What we need is a journey of collaboration. As Bo Prosser puts it,

> In a time in our culture when consumerism is quickly gobbling up resources, the missional family chooses to collaborate and share. Food co-ops, clothes closets and food banks are all ways that we can share from our abundance to help others. The missional family understands that our participation in the reign of God is about sharing our blessings, using wisely the resources available to us and being aware of the needs of those around us.[4]

Diana Garland also gives examples of this from her research and interviews with ordinary families who have found fulfillment, communal strength and Kingdom-focus in her recent book, *Inside-Out Families.*

The Kingdom focus in our marriage relationships and in the way in which we nurture our children invites women and men into a new level of existence, and the gospel announces that this radically different sort of life *is* possible. But what if we, who proclaim the Gospel, don't live it?

What does it mean to actually be Christian together? We are in need of more mentors and role models both for marriage as well as family. In our marriage, my husband and I have learned a lot from the mentoring and modeling of the Benedictine monastics, more specifically from the *Rule of St. Benedict.*[5] For the monastic it's all about collaboration and mutual submission. "The abbot (who oversees the Monastery) represents an outside authority which transcends each individual's own self imposed and often inadequate spiritual system. It is love that impels them

---

4. Prosser, coordinator of Congregational Life for the national Cooperative Baptist Fellowship. bprosser@thefellowship.info.

5. Fry, ed., *RB 1980: Rule of St. Benedict.*

to pursue everlasting life"; so the monastics "no longer live by their own judgment, giving in to their whims and appetites; rather they walk according to another's decisions and directions." The will of God rarely becomes manifest in a vacuum. Most often, it becomes known through people, traditions, teachings, and institutions.[6]

Obedience to the discipline of God's will is our training or *conversatio*,[7] and it shapes us into what we are created to be. Obedience is therefore ultimately freeing, for it takes us out of ourselves and demands that we give ourselves to something greater than self.

Obedience, according to the Rule of Benedict, is not an imposed subservience to an external authority but a condition of inward growth. "Any monk who is not authentically obedient to his abbot and his brethren will not be a happy monk; the carpenter who is not obedient to the laws governing joints will make an unreliable table. All disobedience represents, in this sense, the pursuit of an illusory freedom which obstructs the acquisition of real freedom."[8]

Love without obedience to the limits and rules of conduct is a shallow love, unable to really give except when it meets my needs or makes me feel good.

> Being obedient, whether to God or to my spouse, means doing certain things I sometimes do not feel like doing. It means Bible study and prayer even when I feel I should be off doing something [that may seem more] important [from a cultural perspective]. It means thinking twice about whether or not I really need that enticing purchase. It means balancing my social life with solitude, even when I am frightened of silence. I go against my imme-

6. Taylor, *Spirituality for Everyday Living*, 26 (referring to RB 5.10,12.)

7. One of the Benedictine vows: *Conversatio* is difficult to translate into English but basically means the spiritual process of "sanctification"—a way of life, conduct, behavior, a way in which the monastic is journeying toward Christ-likeness.

8. Dominic Milroy, as quoted in Taylor, *Spirituality for Everyday Living*, 17.

diate feelings and I am obedient to this exterior authority in my life for one reason: I have found that through the limits of obedience I grow beyond the confines of the self with its desires and its traps. Through obedience to the rule, I have found myself obedient in some measure to the will of God.[9]

What does this look like when practically lived out? One personal example from our marriage is when my husband, Dennis, encouraged me to expand my horizons and my calling both spiritually and professionally by applying for a position that would ultimately cause him to give up his tenured position teaching at Wheaton College and follow me out to Southern California. (Granted, some folks, especially those living in SoCal, truly believe that a move from the Midwest to Southern California is a move up; however, for Dennis who honestly believes that Chicago is humanity's greatest accomplishment city-wise, the move both from the city he loved as well as the institution from which he thought he would retire in old age was an act of obedience and submission to my calling.)

He modeled for me, for our children and for many others an act of Christ-like meekness, flexibility and adaptability, and a trust that God was in the midst of this move. And, of course, in retrospect we can look back and see that God had a Kingdom-purpose for Dennis moving to SoCal also. I have to keep reminding him of that!

MOVING FROM SELF-CENTERED, TO COMMUNITY-CENTERED, TO GOD-CENTERED

One of the issues working against authentic obedience in our culture today is that as a whole we no longer have the cultural resources to encourage a mature moral development which equips us to live and model interdependent existence. Lawrence Kohlberg's research on moral development[10] explains our devel-

9. Taylor, *Spirituality for Everyday Living*, 28. Italics mine.
10. Kohlberg, *Moral Development*.

opmental goal should be to move from a level of *ego*-centered or *self*-centered and *self*-serving morality and development to a level of *socio*-centered or *community*-centered morality.

But our cultural condition, as I explained in the first chapter of this book, with our high value on individual rights, consumerism, therapy, and busyness works against this developmental goal. This is exacerbated when "almost one in five American teens say they live with 'hands-off' adults who fail to consistently set rules and monitor their behavior."[11]

Kohlberg's research tells us that our ultimate goal in a truly healthy moral community (or family) should not even be the community centered (socio-centric) one that culturally we often set as the ultimate goal. For the next level up is what Kohlberg calls *theo*centric or *God*-centered, which he also calls principle-centered.

To be specific, when asked the question "Is it wrong to steal?" a person functioning at a self-centered (egocentric) level would respond "no." Why? "Because I want it and I should be able to have what I want." Ask the same question of a person functioning at a community-centered (socio-centric) level and they would respond, "yes." Why? "Because it is not fair to steal" or "because I might get caught and punished." However, an individual functioning at a God-centered/principle-centered (theocentric) level of moral development would answer "yes." Why? "Because it belongs to someone else."

However, the best example of living at a theocentric level of moral development comes from the Old Testament book of the prophet Micah. "What does the Lord require of you?" The prophet responds: "To act justly and to love mercy and to walk humbly with your God" (Mic 6:8, NIV) It is interesting that God gives *some* commands at an egocentric level (e.g., "Thou shall not steal"), still others at a socio-centric level ("Thou shall love your neighbor as yourself"), and a few at a theocentric level (e.g., "Act justly, seek mercy and walk humbly with your God"). This

11. National Center on Addiction & Substance Abuse.

is because God expects us to grow up in our faith and our walk with Him so that we can move from "Thou shalt not steal" to "Seek justice, love mercy and walk humbly with your God." That is partly what the Benedictine vow of *conversatio* is all about.

If our marriages and our families are to be a model for Christ and His Kingdom in this culture we need to be actively concerned not only with our physical, emotional, cognitive, and social development, but also with moral and spiritual development.

MOVING TO RESPONSE-ABILITY
(WHICH LEADS TO PRIVILEGE)

When we teach our fifth grade family *Milestone* at St. Andrew's we include a lesson from Focus on the Family's original *Preparing for Adolescence* curriculum called *The Cycle of Privilege and Responsibility*.[12] This lesson works as well for marriage as for parenting. Basically, if you desire to have more freedom and more respect then you must be willing to show yourself responsible.

I ask the parents and kids to rub their hands together hard and fast. What happens? They get hot. I explain that that's called friction. Friction can create fires that can destroy forests! Friction can also destroy marriages and families! What causes friction? Friction occurs when two objects (or people) push against each other rather than work together.

For example, friction in a family happens when an adolescent wants to have more freedom to make her own decisions, but the parents want to keep control and won't allow her that privilege. When she takes on more responsibility, however, and for example, does her chores without being nagged, she shows respect for her parents. The parents, in turn, allow her more freedom and more privileges that show their respect for her. And so the cycle goes, as long as each family member lives within a paradigm of interdependence by taking responsibility and allowing privilege.

12. Dobson, *Preparing for Adolescence*, 74.

If, however, either falls down on the job, friction occurs and the cycle is broken.

As we practice functioning within a cycle of privilege and responsibility in our marriages and our families as well as in our community, we not only strengthen our family and encourage our children to maturity, we also prepare ourselves to function better within God's Kingdom.

Recall the six definitions of an externally-focused church from chapter two of this book. As we practice interdependence in marriage and family we are better positioned to integrate good deeds and good news into the life of our church and our community.

Interdependence takes work and mutual, conscious effort in marriage and family life. Very little in our media models this value while independence seems the highest goal for advertisers and our politicians.

The best model of interdependence may be a sports team; however, even our professional sports often emphasize individual celebrities over against the team. With the confusion and competition set up between the sexes in the marketplace over the last several decades, a strain is placed on home-life.

As long as we live in competition, we cannot become successfully interdependent. The elevation of women's equal rights, especially in the marketplace, is a good thing and long overdue; however, my point for this chapter is that it often leads to confusion and competition between married couples which can cause tension in relationship and family life. Unless couples and families are intentional in their desire to live a Kingdom lifestyle of mutual support, mutual submission and interdependence in a healthy, Christ-centered marriage and family, the cultural deck is stacked against them.

THE "MEEKNESS" OF WORSHIPING
WITH YOUR CHILDREN IN COMMUNITY

When I was a first-time mother and our son was still a pre-schooler, I already knew that at some point very soon I wanted to introduce our son to the joy of worship in community. I wasn't sure how and when to begin. And, in reality, I was more concerned with what other people in the church sanctuary would think of me than I was with my parenting privilege and responsibility.

One reason that parents often miss the opportunity to introduce their children to worship is that we allow the established church to convince us that our children are a distraction in our worshiping community.

I remember venturing into the sanctuary that Sunday morning with our son Ryan at around three years of age. I'm not really sure if it was more my self-consciousness and fear that he might make a sound or the anticipated glares from others that made me so nervous, but I didn't try that move again for several years. (I love that our congregation at St. Andrew's added "cry rooms" in the back of our sanctuary with comfy rocking chairs and soundproof glass so that families may easily participate in worship. However, I tell parents of older children to be sure to sit toward the front of the sanctuary—near the big cross—so children can be more engaged with the service of worship, instead of sitting in the back with so many other interesting distractions.)

The other reason for missing the opportunity to worship interdependently with our children is that too often our values of individual rights get in the way of our privilege of introducing our children to our heavenly Father in corporate worship.

Too many times I've heard a young parent express frustration that they just want to be able to put their child in someone else's care for an hour so that they might enjoy their quiet (and personal?) time with God in worship. However, this is looking at worship from a consumer worldview, with a cultural "lens" that causes us to ask "what's in it for me?"

One of my favorite books, and one that I wish had been around when our children were young, is Robbie Castleman's *Parenting in the Pew*[13] in which she writes about the joys and benefits of introducing our children to the awe and mystery of our community together in worship. Castleman writes,

> There is a big difference between worship B.C. and A.D.—worship "before children" and worship "after diapers"! I have heard more than a few parents confess, "I used to get more out of church before I had kids." But the bigger issue is, What does God get out of worship? Worship is good for God. Worship concerns itself with his pleasure, his benefit, his good. Worship is the exercise of our souls in blessing God. In the Psalms we read or sing, "Bless the Lord, O my soul!" However, our chief concern is usually "Bless my soul, O Lord!" . . . Children can infringe on our worship experience. I know more than a few parents who have resented the distractions ushered into the pew by the presence of their children. Many just give up. However, children do not have to interfere with *God's* experience of worship! Worship is first a blessing to God, and he values the presence and praise of children (Matt 18:14; Mark 10:14; Luke 18:16). . . . [P]arents in the pew can show by example what it means to seek God, to love his Son and to respond to the Holy Spirit in worship.

How do you know when the time is right to bring your children into "big church" worship? A lot depends on your own attitude and how you convey your own excitement and interest in worshiping to your children. Children between age five and eight can show the most interest in learning about how and why we worship. Also, waiting until a child reaches junior high age may be late for the most meaningful and inquisitive encounter.

You may want to talk with your pastor or Christian educator about arranging a weekday date to take your child into the sanctuary, showing them all the interesting things that are used in your church's worship. Let them stand where the pastor stands,

13. Castleman, *Parenting in the Pew*.

try out the choir loft, explore the sacristy (behind the front platform, where preparation for communion is made and worship equipment is stored).

It is enriching for your child to have a worship tour with your pastor. Not only will the child discover what the worship space is all about, but he or she will begin to form a special bond with the pastor. Parents can help their child think of good questions to ask the pastor about worship services at your church.

For years I have offered a worship workshop for our second grade Family Milestone. In the workshop children and their parents go on a "treasure hunt" throughout the worship space to find all the people, places, and things that help us worship.

When you do decide to bring your child into worship, be sure to plan ahead! Talk about it the week before and plan together. If you're especially organized, you might consider packing a worship bag with items to help make your child's worship more meaningful. Most children would probably love to decide what goes in that bag: perhaps a highlighter to mark when to stand and when to sit in the worship bulletin; perhaps a pad and colored markers for drawing or writing how they feel in worship or their interpretation of the message or the songs. It's probably a good idea to include a pack of Lifesavers candy (after all, being a part of their church family in worship just might "save their lives").

Worshiping with our children and introducing them into the presence of a "Holy other" God can be work. It will take time and preparation and a Kingdom lens that helps us to see why this is important. It can be the most meaningful and interdependent activity we do as a Kingdom-focused family. It is one of the highest means of obedience to the voice and Word of God in *conversatio.*

The A – B – Cs of Worshiping with Children

Arrive at church in time to find a good place to sit. Make sure your children can see. Sit near the front or seat the children on the aisle.

Bathroom visits should be made immediately before entering the worship space. This helps eliminate trips during the worship service.

Crayons, drawing paper, or books will keep your younger child occupied during part of the service. It is too much to ask a child of 5, 6, or 7 to sit and pay attention for the entire service.

Discuss worship at home to prepare children for any departures from the routine of worship (such as Baptism or Communion or other special occasions). Sit aside time to talk about your family worship experience—who, what, when, where and why.

Express your joy at having children worship with you. Send an occasional smile their way. Avoid threats for misbehavior.

Free yourself of anxieties. You are doing what God commands parents to do, training up children in faith.

Give thanks to God for the presence of children.

Help parents of small children by showing your support and appreciation of *our* church's children.

P.S. If you think of it, bring *Lifesavers* for your children to enjoy—being in worship may *save* their *lives*.

Helpful resources for worshiping with children:

Castleman, Robbie. *Parenting in the Pew: Guiding Your Children into the Joy of Worship.* Downer's Grove, IL: InterVarsity, 1993, expanded edition 2002.

Ritchie, James. *Always in Rehearsal: The Practice of Worship and the Presence of Children.* Nashville: Discipleship Resources, 2005.

MOVING FROM "END" TO BEGINNING

In the Rule of St. Benedict the vow of *conversatio* taken by the monastics is a vow of conscious obedience to the voice and Word of God, in order to follow the will of God in all things. The vow of *conversatio*, as I said before, means a way of life, of character development, of conduct and behavior—a way in which the monastic is intentionally being converted into Christ-likeness. "The vow assumes that we are doing our best to progress in perfection in Christ, toward whom we move in our spiritual path. In the baptismal liturgy in our Protestant Book of Common Prayer, it is asked of the candidate: Whenever you fall into sin, will you repent and return to the Lord? *Conversatio* is the vow to do just that in our day-to-day existence."[14]

The vow of *conversatio* is at the root of growth in grace for all Christians. We are all called to take up our cross daily and follow Christ. It is in community, in marriage, and in family and especially with our children that we find the most challenge in this regard.

Other people, especially those we are called to live with on a daily basis, can help us to realize our selfishness and inadequacies. Other people, in their differentness, simply demand by their presence and familiarity that we grow beyond our rigid boundaries.

To truly live our marriage and family in Kingdom focus means that we transform and grow within our situation rather than pulling out and escaping. Living in community with other people (including the community of marriage and family) confronts us with the opportunity to obey, submit, take up our cross *daily*, and become what God desires us to become for His Kingdom purposes.

This is what the apostle Paul talks about in Colossians 3 when he challenges the new Christian believers with a set of rules (or guidelines) for holy living: first set your hearts and minds

14. Taylor, *Spirituality for Everyday Living*, 21.

on God's purpose and stop following the standards of the world; be in unity; dwell in God's Word so you will know how to live together; seek peace; teach and correct one another in wisdom; mutually submit and obey; don't discourage or embitter your children; and work for the favor of the Lord, not of the favor of the world.

Presbyterian minister Penny Hill developed a parenting curriculum about a decade ago (no longer in print) entitled *Parenting for Life* in which she gave some very practical guidelines for living faithfully with our children and biblical models for nurturing them within a Kingdom focused perspective.

In one of the lessons, Rev. Hill suggested making a list of the character qualities each parent in the class would like to see written about their child by a high school guidance counselor for their college application. Parent couples are encouraged to agree on the top three character qualities and then intentionally parent toward that desired end result. As I tell my younger parents in our parent/child program at St. Andrew's, too often we parent with view of the immediate in mind. The immediate reactive mode is that frantic urge us "to get my child in that pre-school," "make sure my child experiences that sport," or "dance class," or "make the social connections at that birthday party." Whereas *proactive* parents begin with a goal and vision in mind of what their child can become as a mature, interdependent adult, and their parenting style and actions reflect that goal.

This relates to discipline as well. Often parents use discipline more as behavior modification and less as discipleship toward the end character quality. We can barely think of our two-year-old as a six-year-old, much less keeping in mind the character we'd desire them to exhibit as they're entering adulthood.

In his book *The 7 Habits of Highly Effective Families*, Stephen Covey gives this sage advice when he writes about *Habit 2: Begin with the End in Mind*.[15] Our parenting goal should be to have a purpose that is bigger than our [immediate] problem. The ob-

15. Covey, *Seven Habits of Highly Effective Families*, 70–111.

jective is to have a clear, compelling vision of what we and our families are all about. When we have our end result clearly in mind, it affects every decision we make along the way.

A clear vision and purpose can override the cultural ethos of individual rights, consumerism and busyness, and keep our marriage and our family on track. Or as Covey says, "Tapping into this sense of vision gives you the power and the purpose to rise above the baggage and act based on what really matters most."[16]

Now the question begs to be asked: What is that end goal that we have for our children? It is one thing to use the advice above to stretch young parents to think and plan beyond getting into the right pre-school or sport or onto the right birthday party e-vite list, by challenging them to think of the character qualities they desire for that child as a graduating senior. But if we are truly seeking to raise children with a Kingdom-focus beyond their individual future plans, we must make the effort to understand just what that end result means.

A very tangible way to do this is to sit down with your spouse (or as a family if your children are old enough to give their input) and create a family mission statement.[17] I have used the exercise of creating a family or a personal mission statement with many of the groups in our ministry, from young couples at a weekend retreat to our sixth graders and parents participating in our sixth-grade Family *Milestone* which we call J.T.M. (Journey Toward Maturity). I've included a sample mission statement in this chapter that you may want to try out.

Creating and sticking with intentional habits and disciplines to move your family toward partnership in Christ's Kingdom is not easy when everyone and everything in our culture pushes against it. That is why just creating a family mission statement is not enough to keep you focused. That is why it is also important to *dwell* within a faith community that knows and cares for each

16. Ibid., 72.
17. See our family mission statement in chapter 4.

other enough to function as the *body of Christ* together to encourage, equip, enable, and empower marriages and families to be what God ordained them to become.

"We can only act within the world we can envision," writes Stanley Hauerwas, "and we can envision the world rightly only as we are trained to see."[18] In other words, it is not the process of a mission statement nor intentionally parenting with the *end results in mind* per se that empowers us. It is having a Kingdom vision of what that end might truly be within the biblical model and mandate. And we receive that biblical mandate when we practice and function within the community of faith where we learn and listen and give and receive witness from that faith community.

For this reason, in addition to creating a mission statement, it is meaningful to our participation in God's Kingdom, as models of God's purpose for marriage and family in the world, to establish a rule of conduct such as St. Benedict provided for the monastics in his order. This rule, when followed within a community, can provide the framework within which to build our vision with God's larger Vision for His Kingdom.

Aside from Dennis Okholm's *Monk Habits for Everyday People: Benedictine Spirituality for Protestants* (of course), there are a few other books published which can provide a model for applying the *Rule of St. Benedict* to marriage and family life. One of my favorites is by Presbyterian pastor, David Robinson, *The Family Cloister: Benedictine Wisdom for the Home.*

---

18. Hauerwas and Willimon, *Peaceable Kingdom*, 29.

Guide for Writing a Marriage/Family Mission Statement

Purpose: To create a clear, easy to follow vision for your life

Step One: *Talk about it:* Where do we hope our marriage/family will be in 10, 25, or 50 years down the road?

How would we like to be remembered and what impact do we hope to have on our children (and our children's children)? On our church? On our community, and the world?

_____

_____

_____

Step Two: *Make a list* to help you explore what your marriage/family is all about.

1. What three words define our marriage/our family?

2. How do each of us define a "successful" marriage? Successful family? _____

3. What role does God have in our marriage and our family? _____

4. What 5 things are truly important to us as a family?

5. What is our highest priority/purpose? _____

6. What principles do we want to teach our children to help them prepare for adulthood and to lead responsible, caring lives? _____

7. Who are our heroes? _____ What is it about them that we like and would like to emulate?

8. What traditions do we want to keep from our families of origin and what sort of traditions would we enjoy creating in our family? _____

_____

_____

9. What does it mean for us to serve in God's Kingdom? (individually; as a couple/family) _____

_____

_____

Step Three: *Write your Family Mission Statement*

- Refine, distill, pull all the ideas together into some kind of expression that reflects your passions, purpose and goals as a couple/a family. *Note*: the fewer words the easier to remember! One sentence or a few bullet points works best.

Step Four: The actual writing is only the beginning. Translate the mission into the fabric of family life, keep it in a visible place in your home. It should carry the power and reminder of shared vision and values. It can keep your marriage and family focused and together, even in the midst of challenge.

(Adapted from Covey, *The Seven Habits of Highly Effective Families.*)

CONVERSATION STARTERS

Focusing Outward: Habits to try on . . .

1. Why do we sometimes say to our spouse or to other people something like this: "You think you have had a busy day. Wait until I tell you about mine!" What causes us to feel a sense of competition even within our marriage relationship? What fosters this desire to outdo one another?

2. Try consciously living with the *cycle of respect and responsibility* in your home. What difference does it make?

Focusing Inward: Family Bible Talk . . .

1. Why does my ego rebel against obedience?

    -   Read Romans 7:15: what causes us to desire to act one way and to do the opposite?

    -   Read Ephesians 6:11–12: how can you and your spouse practice "putting on God's armor?"

    -   Read 1 John 1:9–10: How does this reminder from John remind us of calling on a different kind of strength and power in relationships?

    -   Read Romans 8:28: How does this reminder from Paul encourage you to practice the habit of *beginning with the end in mind?*

2. In what way is God's will made known to you through your family relationships?

3. How might God be using your family to form you into the person he desires you to become?

7

Desperately Seeking Authenticity

Re-Envisioning and Re-Membering

———◆◆◆———

The opposite of remembering is not forgetting, but dis-membering.

—Bruce Waltke

May we choose our rituals more carefully and keep them as full of meaning as possible for as many of our members as possible.

—Gary Parrett & Steve Kang

Unless I call my attention to what passes before my eyes, I simply won't see it.

—Annie Dillard

The way to meet the challenge of spiritual seekers today is through our exceptional living.

—David Martyn Lloyd-Jones

I do believe, help me overcome my unbelief!

Mark 9:24

TRADITIONS AND RITUALS IN A WORLD DESPERATELY SEEKING "AUTHENTICITY"

"We have a hunger for something like authenticity, but are so easily satisfied by an ersatz facsimile."[1] It is sadly interesting that we are so easily swayed by marketing slogans promising something authentic such as the 1999 ad for Winston cigarettes which tried selling us *authenticity* this way: "You have to appreciate authenticity in all its forms." I wonder—even the "authenticity" of a cigarette? It gives pause to wonder about our national obsession for the genuine and authentic! In the marketplace the new sell is authentic: jeans are authentic, soft drinks are authentic, and the church marketers tell us that our worship needs to be authentic. But what is authentic?

In our efforts to sell church to a consumer-minded culture, we hear a lot of authenticity talk coming out of the church in the past few decades. In some contemporary church worship settings the use of church traditions, rituals and even some rites of passage are being left out of the order of worship because, for whatever reason these are considered old-fashioned, out of style, and worst of all, *inauthentic*. The cry goes out that our worship needs to be authentic in order to attract young people, because the media-saturated generations of today are looking for authenticity. The fearful reaction of the local church is that if they don't find it, they'll go elsewhere. And so the church in American culture is suffering from an *authenticity crisis*. Before we can begin to understand the authentic value of traditions, rituals, and rites of passage[2] in our faith formation and that of our children, we

---

1. Orvell, *The Real Thing*.

2. A *ritual* is an action or series of actions that express a belief (for example: the ritual of lighting candles by Acolytes as explained later in this chapter). While a *tradition* is the collective experience upon which a belief is based (for example, the experience of celebrating Christ's birth on December 25). A *rite of passage* marks a unique one-time experience of life such as being confirmed in one's faith or receiving a Bible in worship.

need to take a step back and think about the current state of the church in North American culture.

It is interesting, and somewhat disheartening, to see again how the consumer culture influences us and forms us.[3] Even the concept of authenticity in Christian worship has been reversed to mean new and *individualized* with almost a fear of anything "traditional," versus the definition of authenticity as "historically informed and reenacted." The connotation is so reversed that, as Joshua Glenn puts it, even "authenticity itself has become a kind of ideology . . . [and] one of the most pernicious forms of ideology is 'a vague and noncommittal suspicion of ideology.'"[4] When and why did it become authentic to remove from worship the historically informed worship practices for the perceived sake of being more attractive to a consumer-minded clientele? And, for that matter, is it really authentic to become more like everything else in culture than it is to stand unique and mysterious over against our culturally familiar activities?

When we neglect our historical meta-narrative and allow ourselves and our church's children to be formed outside of that *historically informed Christian meta-narrative*, we risk the free-floating insecurity, so prevalent in our nation today, that lacks a sense of transcendent identity, purpose, and direction. When we forget our traditions and rituals, or worse yet, when the church ignores the authentic traditions and rituals that have been practiced for centuries simply because we don't know why they were ever created in the first place, we dis-member ourselves from our meta-narrative.

By living our Christian marriages and nurturing our own children intentionally within a narrative greater than ourselves

3. See Lee comments (chapter 1) on the values of hyper-individualism in our culture which can be defined in three overlapping moral areas: (1) individual rights; (2) consumerism, and (3) therapy. These all three reinforce the logic of cultural individualism by encouraging and mutually reinforcing what have become ideals for Americans: (1) freedom from constraint, (2) unlimited opportunity and choice, and (3) self-fulfillment.

4. Glenn, "Fake Authenticity," www.hermenaut.com.

and within a community that transcends current media trends, we are held by and developed into the sort of people who are so very much needed in God's Kingdom.

Although media and neo-church leaders want us to believe it, authenticity is not about the latest and newest and most disconnected to the "boring" past. Authenticity is really about something that is authoritative and something that has passed the test of time.

TRADITIONS AND RITUALS:
NOW, TELL ME AGAIN WHY WE DO THAT?

For most people worshiping in North American churches today, it is not that they actually reject the traditions, rituals, and rites of passage that have existed in the church down through the centuries; it is more an issue of not understanding the authenticity of the church's historical traditions and rituals, *why* the church has done these things and *what* bearing these things have, or should have, on our current life situation.

While living in Wheaton, Dennis and I both had our hair cut by a delightful hairdresser who had converted, by marriage, from her Baptist heritage to the Greek Orthodox tradition. Because she desired to understand her new faith tradition better and to make sure that it fit with her commitment to God, her understanding of the Christian faith and the Bible, she set about educating herself in the Greek Orthodox tradition. She studied why the Greek Orthodox Church believed what it believed, and the meanings and purposes behind their particular and numerous rituals.

One day she invited both of us to attend the Orthodox baptism of her first grandson. When we arrived at the church we were handed a sheet of paper on which she had listed each part of the ceremony and the symbolism of each action. This was passed out to everyone in attendance, even those who were brought up in the Greek Orthodox faith.

We probably would have walked away from that service saying to ourselves, "Wow, some of that was weird," had it not been for the written explanation she provided to educate us on the reasons behind each event of that ceremony.

Why do we all—Presbyterians, Catholics, Orthodox, Baptists, etc.—neglect to educate our congregations in our traditions and rituals? Perhaps it is just that people don't have ears to hear (Luke 14:35). I have always appreciated those enriching pastors who take time to pause and explain in the middle of our worship services.

"The spiritual life of the family in first-century Israel was not limited to the small nuclear family unit as we see it today," writes Robert J. Keeley. "The festivals reminding the people of God's faithfulness were national affairs and their celebrations were community events. Both Jesus' family and the larger community took responsibility for his spiritual development."[5]

With American families so isolated from extended family and heritage today, belonging to and connecting with a faith tradition and community takes on a radical importance in giving us and our children the ability to develop our identity, purpose and direction.

CREEDS AND A SENSE OF IDENTITY: WHO AM I?

One of the Family Milestones at our church is giving our third graders their own Bibles in worship. They do a lot of memory work in the months leading up to receiving their Bibles; however, everything that they are encouraged to memorize has a purpose. We talk about *what we believe* as Christ-followers and they are challenged to memorize the Apostle's Creed. We discuss *how we are called to live* as Christ-followers and they work on remembering the ten best ways to live (the Ten Commandments—Exod 20; Deut 5). We teach them about *what we do* as Kingdom people and they memorize *the Shema* (Deut 6:4–9). We find out *how*

5. Keeley, *Helping our Children Grow in Faith*, 25.

we talk to God in prayer and the children learn the Lord's Prayer (Matt 6:9–13). And we discuss *how we enter God's Kingdom,* so they memorize John 3:16 and Revelation 3:20.

During the week before Bibles are presented to the children in our worship services, I take the children and their parents on a *walk through the Bible.* We talk about how their Bible came to be, who wrote it and how it all fits together into one big, overarching story of God's plan for His creation, from the beginning of Genesis to the final Revelation. I love doing this because the parents are also learning something new along with the children. (Frankly, I sometimes wonder how many of the parents ever realized that the Bible is actually a whole story that fits together?)

At the end of the third grade Family Milestone we show a video clip from Worship House Media titled *I Believe,* featuring a combination of the songs "I Believe," by Wes King, and "Creed," by Rich Mullins. I love this short video clip because it reminds us all that the Word of God forms us and makes us who we are. But what is a creed anyway, and how authentic are our creeds?

Our children need to be introduced to the great historical creeds of our faith and begin to understand why we have creeds and what makes them authentic. Our children need to know why is it important to recite creeds when we come together as the family of God to worship and they ought to be able to understand the point in having historical creeds in addition to the Holy Bible. Knowing why we do what we do allows us to be rooted in something deeper than a media-saturated advertisement.

A creed (from the Latin word *credo* meaning "I believe") is simply a statement of what we, as a community, believe. And based on what the community of faith believes, some married couples and families write their own mission statement. It is a popular activity for churches today to take the time to think about and compose a mission statement of their identity and purpose as a church. The foundation of this statement is a creed: to remind us of who we are and what we believe and how we are to live, all written down in a simple, concise statement.

There are some pretty important creeds in the history of our Christian meta-narrative. For example, the Nicene Creed came about from a group of folks in the year 325 AD as they were wrestling with some potential heresies[6] in the church at that time. They gathered in a committee (actually a council) and prayed and wordsmithed together to come up with a definitive statement that summed up what we, as the people of God, believe. It gave us a concise document, easy to remember and easy to repeat.

Another important creed of the historical church was the Barmen Declaration (declaration is another word meaning creed or statement). The Barman Declaration was a creed written by faithful Christians living in Germany during WWII as they courageously stood up to Hitler and reminded the German Confessional Church about its identity and who its true Lord was. (So creeds remind us *who we are* and *what we stand for* in the midst of the prevailing culture.)

Most churches today work together to come up with their own particular, easy to remember and easy to say mission statement, but just think how meaningful and rich it is for *all* Bible-believing churches in our communities and around the world (and down through the church's history) to recite a creed that sums up exactly what we believe as the united followers of Christ? On top of that, just think about what a powerful connectional tool this is when our church leaders (and parents) take the time to explain this to our children. Then our children can experience a sense of identity and a sense of being part of a meta-narrative that is something bigger than "right now."[7]

Another way we express our creed (what we believe) together often on a regular basis in worship (although not often enough

6. The word heresy comes from the Greek word meaning "I choose" and refers to what is not in keeping with the church's historical faith. Heresy usually refers to issues of belief about the Trinity, salvation, or the divinity or humanity of Christ.

7. See chapter 1 on the seven needs of every generation.

in contemporary worship that sometimes ignores 2,000 years of shared memory and tradition) is the regular singing together of the *Gloria Patri* in our worship. This little hymn-creed is the oldest continually sung hymn in our churches. The *Gloria Patri* dates back to the second century. Just imagine: this song has been sung *every* Sunday by at least one church in *every* community all around the world continually for 2,000 years! If that does not give you goose bumps and a sense of connectedness to something so much larger than today's non-denominational churches and worship wars, you may not understand how important this is to our children and our children's children to be connected to the ongoing Story and Vision.[8]

BLESSINGS AND A SENSE OF PURPOSE: DO I BELONG TO A BIGGER STORY?

Another tradition to give our children a true concept of authenticity as well as to give them "roots and wings," goes back to the Old Testament world and the concept of giving a blessing. There are many examples in the Bible of people conveying God's blessing to others. Perhaps the most famous is the blessing given by Moses to Aaron and his sons (Num 6:22–27). Blessings can connect with our children on many levels.

I am invited by our parent/child program[9] director at St. Andrew's to meet with the parents in that program a couple of sessions each year. I talk with the parents about the importance of prayer and teaching their children to pray. One of the ideas that I share with them is "Giving your child a blessing." I love hearing the different stories from the parents about how they were given blessings or intentionally give blessings to their children. One mother told of her father always giving a blessing by the front door as children left home. As she was leaving for a date during high school years she remembered her father putting his hand on

---

8. See chapter 4 on developing a sense of purpose and direction.
9. St. Andrew's weekday program for 12–36 month olds and their parents.

her head and saying something like, "May you always know that God is with you and watching over you wherever you go, may you do nothing that would dishonor Him." That may give a teenager pause during the evening events, though of course, as I told her, that would have to be a practice begun when she was just a child; to throw that one at your teenager without an established history could really backfire! Another example of a blessing is the mother who got an idea while changing children's bed sheets and flipping mattresses. She invited her small children (aged 5, 4, and 2) to come into their rooms where she took permanent marker and wrote permanent prayers for them on the slats of their bed frames—even on the toddler's crib! Those three kids (at least the two oldest ones) could tell me exactly what their mom did and what that means to them to know her prayer blessing is written on their bed frames.[10]

10. You can visit this mom's blog about raising faithful kids at www.bringingupburns.com.

126

Another way to give a blessing can easily be incorporated into congregational worship. I first saw this at Holy Family Catholic Church in Inverness, Illinois[11] and loved it so much that I incorporated it into our St. Andrew's worship when I joined the staff a decade ago. We've used it ever since and now have raised up a generation of children who have experienced this regular blessing each week in worship. After I call the children to the front during worship services and give a brief children's message, I then ask the children to stand for our "blessing." They raise their right hand in blessing and say to the congregation: "May the Lord be with you as you worship Him." Then the congregation has been trained to raise their right hands to the children and say, "And may the Lord be with you as you learn to follow Him." Such practices remind our children who they are and whose they are as they go out of the sanctuary to their classes.

The giving and receiving of blessings can enrich our lives as a family and as a church family at times when a prayer is not easy to say—at the bedside of an ill parent or grandparent, when a child is afraid or insecure, or even in a sticky note attached to the inside of a school notebook for a school age child before a big test. It can also be a Kingdom-focused message to friends and relatives. I heard a story of a father and mother delivering their daughter to her college dorm for the first time. As the parents headed back to the car in the parking lot without their daughter, feeling a bit anxious and lonely, their daughter stuck her head out the dorm room window and yelled, "Hey, mom and dad, you forgot to give me my blessings!" How rewarding to head back into that dorm room at the daughter's bidding to give that precious blessing and to know that she'd been given a heritage that could not be easily torn down.

11. www.holyfamilyparish.org.

SERVICE AND A SENSE OF COMMUNITY: WHAT IS MY PLACE? TO WHOM AM I ACCOUNTABLE?

In many churches around the world and down through the ages, there have been children and youth who have served to "bring in the light," the Bible, banners, and crosses in order to enhance corporate worship services. Traditionally these acolytes, as they're called, have worn robes or cowls. Often in our contemporary worship services and in our constant awareness of making our worship culturally sensitive, the historical and truly authentic practice of using acolytes has been dropped. However, this activity and service has a rich tradition in our worship that can not only bless our congregation but give purpose and place to our children in taking their particular place in leading our corporate worship (and there is simply no reason why it could not, with a little thoughtful creativity, be incorporated into our contemporary worship spaces).

When I train the new acolytes at St. Andrew's each fall I begin by telling them the story of one of the first recorded acolytes in history: the Old Testament story of the boy Samuel. This also serves to move them beyond simply a life application of the story of Samuel to put them *into* Samuel's story that they now have the privilege of continuing. I challenge them to tell me what acolytes do in worship, why they do it and, most of all, the symbolism of their service for the family of God in worship. And they explain to me that the flames of the torch[12] and candles symbolizes Christ's light in the world. As they carry the torch into our worship and light the candles they can tell me that they are symbolically reminding our church family that Christ is present and that His word will be proclaimed today. As they carry in the large sanctuary Bible they remind the congregation of the importance of the scripture in our lives (that also gives us light for our daily paths). As they come back into the sanctuary at the end of our

12. The word "torch" is the name commonly given to the long wand used to light the candles.

worship they relight the torches and "hush"[13] the candles, and then carry the light back down the aisle and out of the sanctuary, they understand that they are symbolically carrying the light back out into the world. With a few words of explanation, this also serves as a reminder to our congregation that they are also responsible to carry the light out into the world all week long, until they come back together again in worship. Our acolytes also carry in a cloth that is placed under the Bible on the communion table. The cloths are in different colors and many of our St. Andrew's children can tell you that each color represents a different season of our church year calendar. But just having acolytes serve in worship is not enough. The act must be explained to our children and to our adults who have forgotten (or most likely never knew) why we do this.

Like all traditions in our worship, if no one takes the time to explain why we do what we do, it loses its authenticity and its power to shape our lives. Having children and youth as acolytes in a worship service can easily be a missional activity when we allow it to become special and meaningful and unique in our world.

RITES OF PASSAGE AND A SENSE OF PURPOSE: WHY AM I HERE?

Kang and Parrett explain that "in Jewish tradition, rites of passage have been integral to education and formation and tied to a child's growth in wisdom."[14] In Catholic tradition, as well, rites of passage have long been a critical component of one's spiritual formation. In fact, the seven sacraments recognized in the Church of Rome are tied to key rites of passage in the life of an individual. Many evangelicals have rejected such practices as unnecessary or even unhealthy. But such an attitude simply betrays, once

---

13. "Hush" is common terminology for putting out the flame on the candles. Learning the traditional terminology helps make acolyting unique and more meaningful for our children.

14. Kang and Parrett, *Teaching the Faith, Forming the Faithful*, 330.

more, our lack of wisdom and education about why we do these things. Where we fail to provide or give shape to meaningful and intentional rites of passage for our children, the surrounding market-driven culture will rush in with alternatives to fill the void. In his study of the American culture of divorce, Andrew Cherlin reminds us: "Ritual assures that people will remember and belong. Traditional wedding ritual reminds everyone in the congregation of their own vows. [However] it could be that, despite the efforts of the wedding industry, the need for a highly ritualized ceremony and legalized status will fade. And there is not much else supporting marriage in the early 21st century."[15] As well, Kang and Parrett note that,

> Thus we in North America have been shaped by the powerful social rituals surrounding a young girl turning "sweet sixteen." The prom for high-schoolers, engagements to be married, the multibillion-dollar wedding industry, the multibillion-dollar baby industry, and on and on. The need for meaningful rites of passage is inherent in our humanity, and the church is wise to address it. Thankfully, many evangelical churches have shown signs of helping us correct course in this regard.[16]

What fun it has been over the years for me, as a church educator, to introduce parents and their children to unique, one-time-only rites of passage. As I've already written about in several previous chapters, these "Family Milestones," as we call them, offer a distinctive milestone for each age level on an annual basis. The milestone for our first graders and their parents takes place the Sunday afternoon right before the new church year beings.[17] After we share fellowship around a lunch together,

15. Cherlin, "Disinstitutionalization of American Marriage," 857.

16. Kang and Parrett, *Teaching the Faith, Forming the Faithful*, 331.

17. The "Church year" begins with the first Sunday of Advent as opposed to the "Julian Calendar" followed in our culture, which begins on January 1. (Our calendar today is based on the "Julian Calendar" introduced in 46 BC by Julius Caesar as a reform of the Roman calendar. Ironically, many of the months are named after pagan deities.)

the parents and their children go on a "walk through the Church Year." We introduce the lesson by showing examples and talking about calendars: "What special days do we have marked on our American calendar that are celebrated only in our nation (e.g., Independence Day, President's Day)? If you check out the calendar, you'll find more. When we mark these dates on our calendars and celebrate them, they make us and form us into who we are: Americans! It makes us know that we are unique as members of our nation." Then I show them calendars of other nations (perhaps a French calendar and a Romanian calendar) and talk about the holidays that remind those citizens of who they are as the French or the Romanians. Finally, I introduce them to our church calendar.

I say to the first graders and their parents, "Notice that our church calendar begins with the first Sunday in Advent, not on January 1; that's when the new church year begins. We have purple weeks (four of them before Christmas and six before Easter, so that when we see purple on our calendar or in our worship we know that we're getting ready for something important in our church). Then we count the white weeks and talk about why they're white. We check out the only red week on our church calendar and talk about what that week means (Pentecost—which we also refer to as "the birthday of the Church"). Then there are all those green weeks; green reminds us of growing and reminds us of our need to grow in our faith and in the knowledge of our place in God's family."[18]

18. I use the Church Year model from Stewart & Berryman's *Young Children in Worship*.

The Church Year Calendar

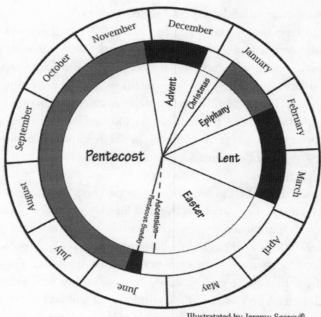

Illustratated by Jeremy Searcy©

At the end of our first grade Family Milestone our children and their parents take home their new church year calendars (we add family activities to each month) and they also take home a special white "Christ candle" that they can light at home each week or each month on special holy days in our church year, to remind the family regularly of how celebrating our church year makes them special and also reminds them they are part of God's family and part of God's Story down through history.

I am saddened that so many American Christians invest so much time and effort decorating their homes or throwing parties to remember who they are as Americans while they remain totally ignorant of their rich heritage and history as citizens of God's Kingdom. As David B. Batchelder writes, "Without a

Christian calendar functioning in the festive life of a family, the landscape of family celebration will be filled with whatever our cultural calendars have to offer."[19]

Speaking at our women's retreat a few years back, Marva Dawn reminded us that the church year with its seasons allows us to keep our focus on God. The result of worship is that we should be equipped to bring the Good News of salvation to others. However, sometimes our worship (in the local church) has this reversed. Worship becomes a tool to evangelize rather than equip the believers to share their faith. When the two are confused, the worship becomes centered on the one being evangelized and loses its proper center on God.

Participation in corporate worship and celebrating rituals and traditions of our historical church is a means to restore our vision—a means to help us see what the prevailing culture has discouraged us from seeing. It is also a way to be truly authentic.

INTENTIONALLY CELEBRATING OUR FAMILY'S AUTHENTICITY

Another way in which each marriage and family can establish and celebrate events and seasons that make them unique and connect them to a sense of their own family history is to mark special events with one's own signature. Many families celebrate a family member's baptism date each year by lighting a special candle at the dinner table or, perhaps, looking at pictures or talking about ways that family member has grown in faith and served in God's Kingdom over the past year.

Diana Garland talks about the Kingdom-focus of intentionally celebrating our "faith-families" and "faith-parents" who nurture us in faith in our church communities. She writes:

> Once faith-family relationships develop they need to be named and celebrated, wrapped about with community recognition and blessing. For example, rather

19. Batchelder, *Home as Family Church*, 165.

than celebrating our culture's Mother's Day and Father's Day—which exclude many [members of our church family]—congregations can celebrate Faith-Mother's Day and Faith-Father's Day . . . Congregational members can find ways to recognize those who have mothered and fathered them in the faith.[20]

Family mealtimes can also become a special family tradition: the way it is served, who cleans up, how conversation is carried on, a review of each person's day, an opportunity for a short Bible and/or devotional reading and family prayer. Even the prayer can become a forming tradition. As our children were growing up we always sang the first stanza to a meaningful hymn of thanksgiving by a German pastor in the 1600s named Martin Rinkert. It gave us the opportunity not only to teach ourselves a hymn, but it also gave us opportunity to help our children understand and remember that Rinkert wrote the hymn in the middle of the European Thirty Years War and in the midst of a dire famine that had claimed the lives of many of his parishioners, including his wife and several of his children. Yet in the midst of all this, he still wrote this hymn as a table blessing for his remaining family and church family to sing together to be reminded of God's faithfulness.[21] Singing the first stanza of this hymn together each evening at dinner helped to form and connect our family in something truly authentic for us. What a joy it was recently to sit at the dinner table of our daughter and her husband along with our six month old granddaughter and have them hold hands around their dinner table and lead us in singing this hymn together in their home.

Another special way to give children and marriage partners a deeper and richer sense of purpose and identity is to tell and retell the stories of family. "Remember the time that Grandma did this or Uncle David did that? Did you know that your great-great-great grandfather was . . . ?" This is much more meaningful

20. Garland, *Family Ministry*, 375–76.
21. Rinkert, "Now Thank We All Our God."

to do at least one meal per week instead of watching the TV or playing video games while wolfing down a fast food meal.

Bruce Waltke reminds us that "we have effectively dismembered our children by stripping them of the memories they so desperately need."[22] The words "dis-membering" and "re-membering" are powerful word pictures of what we do to our marriages and our families when we are not intentional about reminding ourselves that we are members of something so much bigger and more important than our daily duties in life. Every time we tell the stories of our family and the stories of the people of God—our great-grandparents of faith down through church history—we are in effect *re-membering* ourselves to our true identity, purpose, and direction in life.

A HOUSE IS FURNISHED WITH FURNITURE; A HOME IS FURNISHED WITH MEMORIES[23]

The way we think of our home—either as a place to showcase as a designer's model home or as a place of re-membering and forming ourselves and our children—bears impact on our identity, our purpose and the direction of our lives. Perhaps there is too much pressure on couples starting out today to have it all. If they do not decorate their home and have all the coordinating colors and furniture they start off feeling as though they're not successful, when in reality beginning housekeeping with a hodge-podge of hand-me-downs might be just the thing to help them begin to establish priorities and meaningfulness in their new home. A question to ask each other might be: What shapes our identity as a family? Is it our acquisitions, or is it by defining our place and purpose in a larger story than right here and right now?

In one of our family's favorite movies, *SweetLand*,[24] the memory of the farmer's grandparents' sacrifice and hardships to

22. Waltke, *Way of Wisdom from the Book of Proverbs.*
23. Garland, *Family Ministry,* 376.
24. Selim, *Sweetland.*

make the farm what it is today led him to make an ethical decision not to sell his land to a developer (and therefore to resist the pull of consumerism). In other words, remembering the story in which one's life is located dictates the kinds of decisions and actions one must make in the world. In the movie, the young man was tempted to "dis-member," but in "re-membering" he was able to act according to the narrative that had shaped his life.

MISSION WITHIN A GREATER COMMUNITY AND A SENSE OF DIRECTION: WHERE AM I GOING?

When our children were young, and partly because we lived so far from our extended family, we would look for a ministry to visit and serve on holidays such as Thanksgiving, Christmas, or Easter. Our favorite was Emmaus Ministry on the north side of Chicago.[25] Sometimes we'd prepare and bring the meal or part of the meal; other times, as the ministry grew in numbers, we'd simply show up and help prepare the meal. We would spend time talking and singing and sharing our lives with the men who showed up, as well as distributing Christmas gifts from our church in the suburbs. This simple one-day mission had a life-forming impact on our children, especially on our daughter, who decided to spend a college semester living and taking classes at the Emmaus facility.

Although we would not recommend other families do anything quite so radical, when our children were in elementary school we spent six weeks one summer teaching and serving with Nile Theological College students in Khartoum, Sudan (Africa). It was indeed a life-forming experience for us all.[26] Our children gained a richer understanding of their Christian family as it exists in another culture, the impact of persecution, and what it means

25. Emmaus Ministries was started by two of Dennis' former Wheaton students, John and Carolyn Green as a way to share the Gospel with gay prostitutes on the streets of Chicago. www.streets.org.

26. See Nile Theological College at www.pcusa.org/worldwide/globaled/nile.htm.

to live in a very different culture than their own. Although, as I said, we'd not recommend to anyone else to take their children into a terrorist nation (it was declared that by the U.S. soon after we returned back home!), we do recommend to parents regularly to take advantage of mission and service opportunities they can participate in locally. Many of our St. Andrew's families go to Tecate, Mexico for a weekend of building and playing with the boys at Rancho San Juan Bosco Orphanage.[27] Others serve locally with various ministries in our area. The point is not only to send money or to bring an offering for missions to Sunday School, but to work and serve alongside members of God's family (both from our church and from our partner's in Mexico) who can form us and our children and create an external focus that honors and enriches God's Kingdom.

"Adults who can remember as a child (aged five to twelve), doing something for others with their parents," says Merton P. Strommen, "show significantly higher faith scores than those who cannot remember being involved in this way. Parents who both verbalize and live their faith establish a quality of family life that is encouraging."[28]

DON'T LET ME LOSE MY WONDER AND A SENSE OF POWER AND HOPE: CAN I SURVIVE?

We cannot simply describe for our children the community of faith, the body of Christ or a love for God that transcends all barriers to embrace neighbors of all kinds, and expect that this will become a part of their reality. Therefore, we must allow them the opportunity to experience such a community for themselves—an inclusive community of memory bound together by the Holy Spirit. "They need to *see* and *hear* and *feel* such a community in operation before they will be able to embrace this alternative vision of reality. Where, apart from congregational worship, do

---

27. See Rancho San Juan Bosco, www.rsjbkids.com.
28. Strommen, "Rethinking Family Ministry," 70–71.

children have an opportunity to experience the community in all (or at least much) of its diversity?"[29]

Since a majority of ministries segregate by age, interest, theological persuasion, gender, or marital status, we seldom find ourselves in groupings that are more representative of the faith community at its most diverse than we do in worship (though, unfortunately, worship services are often segregated, even by generation).

When we seek creative ways of allowing our children and youth to participate in our corporate worship, they learn to see a world beyond their understanding. My friend Robbie Castleman authored *Parenting in the Pew,* in which she talks about preparing our children for worship and experiencing it through their eyes. One of my favorite quotes from Robbie is this: "Modern people worship their work, work at their play and play at their worship." She goes on to remind her readers that "worship is hard work, especially with our children, but it is so worth it to create in our children a sense of wonder and a sense of belonging."[30]

Tony Campolo talks about the importance of our traditions in worship. He says that "those who are most committed to their church learn to value high liturgy and ritual as ways to express and live in their faith; whereas those who are least committed to their church and their faith prefer low or no ritual."[31]

Tony gives an example of a charismatic preacher in the local church in which the worship revolved around his funny and memorable sermons:

> The people came to hear, to be entertained and to be challenged by his messages, all wonderful, of course and what we value in our preachers. However, when that preacher left, the church falls apart. But in the Catholic

---

29. Ritchie. *Always in Rehearsal,* 26.

30. Castleman, *Parenting in the Pew,* 43.

31. Tony Campolo. *Traditions: The Key to a Close Knit Family,* podcast.

church it doesn't matter so much who the priest is, it is the tradition and liturgy that holds people together![32]

I would, of course, prefer to suggest that we learn to value our traditions and nurture our children to appreciate what we do and why they form us, and also have that charismatic preacher! Still, Campolo makes his point.

As Tevya reminds us in *Fiddler on the Roof*, tradition lets us know who we are and how to live. Traditions keep us loyal, make us belong, give us emotional well being. Tradition reminds us how we are to live our lives in the world and the reason we are who we are as disciples of Christ. Traditions are rarely manifested in age-segregated, developmentally appropriate settings. Rituals are how God works to form us and connect us and *re-member* us in family and community. Rituals are crucial to the solidarity of any group. Ritual is what keeps the family together.

In the sacrament of communion, Jesus said, "I want you to eat this bread and drink this cup, for as often as you do you will *remember*." It is not the remembering that leads us to the ritual. As Campolo puts it, it is the ritual that keeps us remembering.

> You show me a church that forgets to celebrate communion and I'll show you a church who forgets the centrality of Jesus Christ. And in a church that celebrates only twice or so per year the people will forget. Show me a family with a high level of ritual and I'll show you a healthy family.[33]

Dennis and I, even when we first married, planned carefully to intentionally create our own family traditions around our major celebrations: Christmas, Easter, anniversaries, as well as our minor celebrations such as eating dinner as a family, even when we were only a family of two! And now when our children are grown, we are amazed when they reflect those traditions back to us. We realize just how much those intentional family rituals and

32. Ibid.
33. Ibid.

traditions formed our children. On one recent Thanksgiving, our daughter Emily flew home for a brief visit while her husband, Keith, attended to ordination requirements out of town. She was particularly excited to be with us for our "first Sunday in Advent" tradition of putting up the Christmas tree, transforming the house for Advent and Christmas, baking cookies, pouring the egg nog, sitting by the lighted Christmas Tree and listening to Manheim Steamroller's rendition of *Silent Night*—just as we had done all her years of growing up (and which was instituted by us as a couple before our children were born).

One Sunday at St. Andrew's, after a communion service, one of our members and mother of three boys greeted me in tears as she was coming out the door of the sanctuary. "What's wrong, Gabriella," I asked her. "These are tears of joy!" was her answer. She explained how moving it had just been for her to share communion with her sons after preparing them the day before for communion. The back story is that on the weekends in which we invite children to join their parents in the holy act of communion at St.Andrew's Church, I send out an e-mail blast as a reminder to the parents of our older elementary age and junior high age youth, attaching a guide for them to go over with their children about the sacrament of communion. That weekend Gabriella and her husband Jeff had taken that guide and talked it over with their sons, and the next morning they shared the Lord's Supper together in worship. This experience of sharing the Lord's Supper together was between brothers and their sister in Christ, not only between mother and father and sons. No amount of teaching in the Sunday school classroom could have accomplished what that simple e-mail had done for the Christian education of that family.

What we do to train our church's children and to empower families in faith must move outside the twentieth-century paradigm of professional youth ministry or professional children's ministry. Ben Walker, a youth minister at Northern Hills Christian Church Cincinnati, Ohio, writes about revelations that came to him during college days. Ben said that he often found himself alone in taking a stand for Christ in his college classes and wondering what ever happened to all those fine Christian students that our churches sent off to the universities? "Where are the believers who are ready to destroy speculations and every lofty thought raised up against the knowledge of our God?" Ben wondered, "And where are our disciples?" Ben suggests that the answer to that may be easy given the way the church has usually run youth groups for our teens over the past half century.

> They're primed and ready to put into practice that which we've [the church/youth groups] discipled them in: opening bananas with their toes and playing hockey with paper plates. Or perhaps our young world-changers are exploring how many Vienna sausages they can fit in their respective mouths. We can also say our students are apt at achieving emotional highs and have a distinct capacity to get fired up in a worship setting—or at least can fake that passion. Yes, these are our disciples. Armed to the teeth with—what? The experience of inane pep-rallies and rudimentary knowledge of the Scriptures? (Scriptures, I should add, that are viewed as devoid of authority outside of Christian circles.) Look out, world!

It is true that in the way we've raised children and youth in North American churches over the last few decades that we have set a "fire of passion" in our youth at conferences, retreats, camps, and youth worship services. But is that enough? "Can you imagine a boot camp where soldiers are trained to go into combat and the primary training method is building troop morale? Imagine what happens to those soldiers when they are sent into real combat without weapons, or any idea how to use weapons. I suspect the efforts of many brave soldiers would end ineffectually, but most would engage in a very rational desertion."[34]

Through the intentional process of understanding and *actively* participating in the traditions, rituals, and rites of passage of the faith community, our children begin to know that they

---

34. Walker, "More than Fun and Games," accessed online.

belong to something bigger and deeper than any other part of their daily lives.

As we talk about our faith traditions and encourage our kids to bring in their perspective they begin, not to own their own faith, but they begin to own the *church's* faith. As we share our stories of our faith journeys and the stories of our church rituals that have the power to *re-member* us with past and present Christian communities and our children are better equipped to carry that faith out into their world.

With your family you might consider taking intentional moments to reflect on the awe and wonder of the mystery that is at the core of our faith. With all that we see displayed before our eyes in the media, very little is amazing to us anymore, and yet the awe and wonder of belonging to a "holy other" God has that power to humble and amaze us as no 3D movie ever can. Think about and reflect on the traditions and creeds that form and have formed you and your family as you become an authentic reflection for God's Kingdom in the culture.

St. Andrew's Presbyterian Church Family Milestones

Kindergarten Family Milestone
A transition from pre-school to elementary school for new Kindergarteners and their parents.

1st Grade Family Milestone
Families explore the different seasons and special days of our church year together. Each family takes home a "Christ Candle" to use for family devotions and their own copy of the church year calendar.

2nd Grade Family Milestone
Families explore our worship sanctuary or "big church" and all that we do together as we worship God.

3rd Grade Family Milestone
3rd graders receive a Bible in front of our church congregation in worship. A series of classes and family Bible workshop give an opportunity for the 3rd grader and his/her parents to learn about their new Bibles.

4th Grade Family Milestone
Families learn about the sacraments of our church.

5th Grade Family Milestone
As children approach the age of adolescence, the church offers a 6-week series for kids along with their parent(s) facilitates open communication for many years to come.

6th Grade Family Milestone
Journey Toward Maturity (J.T.M.) offers weekly classes for 6th graders with their parents. What is begun in this class is followed up in Jr. and Sr. High years.

CONVERSATION STARTERS

Focusing Outward: Habits to try on . . .

1. Take a look at the Church year calendar I've provided in this book and see if you can discover new celebrations to take on as a couple/as a family to help you better identify with your Christian heritage.

2. Consider intentionally participating in one or two rituals within your church's tradition and talk about how they develop a deeper identity, purpose and direction within God's ongoing story of faith and redemption.

Focusing Inward: Family Bible Talk . . .

Look at the following Bible passages and creeds. Use the discussion questions to get a conversation started about your family identity, purpose, and direction:

1. **What we believe** (read The Apostle's Creed)

    I believe in God, the Father Almighty, the maker of heaven and earth, and in Jesus Christ, his only son, our Lord: who was conceived by the Holy Spirit, born of the virgin Mary, suffered under Pontius Pilate, was crucified, dead, and buried; he descended into hell. The third day he rose again from the dead; he ascended into heaven, and is seated on the right hand of God the Father Almighty; from there he will come again to judge the living and the dead. I believe in the Holy Spirit; the holy catholic[35]church; the communion of saints; the forgiveness of sins; the resurrection of the body; and the life everlasting.

---

35. The word *catholic* (with a small "c") means universal.

- Why do you think that it is valuable to have a creed to live by?

- What are the most important things for us to believe as a couple/as a family and why?

2. **How we live** (read The Ten Commandments— Exod 20; Deut 5) also called the ten best ways to live.

    - Does it make a difference in your appreciation of the 10 commandments if your think of them as "the 10 Best Ways to Live"?

    - How do creeds and rituals in your church help you to better obey and live out the 10 Commandments in your family?

3. **What we do** (read the *shema*—Deut 6:4–9)

    - Why did God give this instruction to the Hebrew people?

    - Put this message into your cultural language and discuss what acting this out might look like in the context of your daily family life.

4. **How we talk to God** (read the Lord's Prayer— Matt 6:9–13)

    - Does it help your family prayer time to know that God gave you a model for prayer? Try putting this prayer into your own language and cultural setting.

    - Think about some other meaningful ways to pray including the giving of a blessing (see the *Seven Creative Ways to Pray with Your Children* in chapter 5 of this book).

5. **How we enter the Kingdom of God** (read John 3:16 and Rev 3:20)

- Reread the quote from Ben Walker earlier in this chapter. Talk about this: how do we communicate the plan or path of salvation to ourselves, our children and our community? Is our goal to live anyway we want to now as long as we have our "ticket to Heaven"?

- What does John mean in the famous Bible verse (John 3:16) when he writes about everlasting life? Does he mean life in the future or is he talking about the way we can live our life right in the "here and now"?

8

Radically Rooted

Re-Envisioning Stability and Balance in Kingdom Family

Grow us slowly, persistently, and deeply, Lord, to be people who watch without distraction, listen without interruption, and stay put without inclination to flee. Amen.

— Shane Claiborne, Jonathan Wilson-Hartgrove, and Enuma Okoro

Without change and growth, stability is a prison, without stability, change is chaos. Without mutual commitment, obedience is slavery, and without obedience to a higher authority, change is capricious.

— Anonymous

Wherever I am, at home, in a hotel, in a train, plane or airport, I would not feel irritated, restless, and desirous of being somewhere else or doing something else. I would know that here and now is what counts and is important because it is God himself who wants me at this time and in this place.

— Henri Nouwen

I am the vine; you are the branches. If you remain in me and I in you, you will bear much fruit; apart from me you can do nothing.

John 15:5

RADICALLY ROOTED AND GROUNDED

"*Radical*, in its origins, really means to *be rooted*."[1] The idea behind the word is to be so grounded, so deeply rooted in a lifestyle direction, that one is able to stand firm within the social and cultural whirlwinds that sweep others off course. "Today, anyone who adheres to the person and teachings of Christ in the midst of runaway humanism and hedonism is, by definition, a radical."[2]

Being radically rooted serves as an object lesson for the spiritual discipline of stability. Stability gets a bad rap these days. It often connotes images of being stuck in a rut or, worse yet, boring. When did being a stable human being get to be a negative within our culture? Perhaps it is because the stars of Hollywood and sports that we have come to idolize are usually thought of as radical and exciting, free flowing, shocking, and anything but stable. However, the idea of a stable marriage or stable family in our world today *is* something radical. Or as Will Willimon and Stanley Hauerwas put it, "These days, just one person running loose in southern California who keeps the sixth commandment is enough to attract a crowd. Call it ordinary folks like us getting to be saints."[3]

FULLY COMMITTED

The vow of stability is the first of the vows in Benedict's *Rule* for his monks. Perhaps that is because even in the fifth century Benedict knew that nothing is possible until we give over our entire life to the primacy of God's Kingdom. "If we leave ourselves an escape hatch we have one foot out the door, and we are not fully committed,"[4] whether that be a commitment to the monastery, to a community, or to a marriage.

---

1. Barrett, "Searching for Radical Faith," accessed online.
2. Ibid.
3. Hauerwas and Willimon, *Truth About God*, 102–3.
4. Brian Taylor, *Spirituality for Everyday Living*, 7.

"If we say to ourselves that we will stay committed as long as commitment stays exciting and devoid of suffering, we are not fully committed. What does that internal commitment do for me and others? What happens to monk or marriage partner who cannot continue in stability, or who seems to be called out of it? How is grace experienced when failure to be fully committed occurs?"[5] For the Benedictine monk, the vow of stability is a commitment to stay with the same community for the rest of one's life.

In a marriage relationship, the vow of stability should also be a part of our conscious and verbal commitment to our spouse to remain faithful for a lifetime. We usually say it in our marriage vows: "in sickness and in health, till death do us part." But many people, including many Christians, don't take that vow all that seriously. The vow of stability, along with two other vows, (obedience—see chapter 6—and *conversatio*, which, though difficult to translate into English, basically means a spiritual process of growing in Christ-likeness), are taken by a monk as he enters into a covenantal relationship with the monastic community.

These vows form the basis of a life-long commitment that grounds (or roots) the monk to something deeper and more profoundly radical than life lived outside the community. But what do these same vows mean for marriage partners?

I wonder what would happen if ordinary folks entered the holy covenant of marriage with the same conviction and the same covenantal vows as monks? Or if, in the conscious act of starting a family and training faithful children, Christ-following parents could step back for a long view of the privileged relationship of partnership with God in forming a new being and take those vows before God and community to provide for stability, provide

---

5. Ibid. (Note: Grace extended to our brothers and sisters in Christ and to those outside the Kingdom who are suffering in unhealthy relationships is, of course, what we are commanded to provide; however, that is not the subject for this chapter and will not be explored here.)

for growth in a faith community (*conversatio*), and model faithful acts of obedience?

My daughter, who at the time had been married for only five years, shared with me a conversation that she's had with her hairdresser. The hairdresser was amazed that Emily had been married *so long*. Emily went on to tell me about a colleague who, in conversation with a young woman, mentioned that he'd been married for twenty-seven years, to which the young woman exclaimed, "Wow! I've never known anyone who was married that long! It must really be working for you!" When he asked how long she expected to be married, her answer was "about ten years"—she hoped!

To many young people today, the idea of a truly long-term relationship is something radical. As Christ-followers wouldn't it be amazing if we could witness to a longing world the stability and obedience necessary to remain in a faithful relationship?

TAKING VOWS . . . INTENTIONALLY

Back in the early 1970s when Dennis and I were a young, engaged couple we both decided to take summer school courses at California state universities during our summer break from Wheaton College. Wanting to complete our psychology requirements, we both signed up for summer "encounter groups."[6] Both of us, at separate Southern California universities, experienced the same incredulous responses from members of our groups when we talked about our commitment to one another for life.

Even back then, forty years ago, the expectation was that marriage would, *of course*, not last a lifetime and the students in our encounter group class considered us young and naive to think that it would. For us, however, even at the ripe old ages of 20 and 21 at that time, the vows we were taking left us convinced

6. An encounter group was a form of group psychotherapy that emerged with the popularization of humanistic psychology in the 1960s. The work of Carl Rogers (founding father of *person-centered psychotherapy*) was central to this movement.

that this was a "till death do us part" commitment. We took it very seriously and we still do. That does not mean that God cannot and will not work in the life of someone who finds they are in a wrong and unhealthy relationship; but what it *does* mean is that for most of us, if we are committed to be part of God's Kingdom purpose, we should enter a marriage relationship for the long haul.

Just as Israel and Yahweh (who demonstrated a relentless faithfulness) are models of marriage relationship, perhaps our Christian marriages ought to be encouraged by the acts of God and Israel, and the acts of Jesus Christ and the church, to have the courage and conviction to be a model of something more than the culture expects.

OUT OF BALANCE AND RESTLESS

If you're old enough, you'll remember LP records. If you're into retro you're probably collecting them today. They usually worked pretty well unless they were scratched badly or unless that little hole right in the center had been cut slightly off-center.

If you have ever tried to play an LP with the center hole off-center, you'll know that it does not work so well. A vinyl record or any sort of a wheel with the center "off" gives a good object lesson for a life that is out of balance. To have balance and harmony in my life and my marriage I must continually seek to stay centered. To stay balanced and centered means that I have my priorities rightly ordered. It is a conscious and daily decision to put first things first in life.

In his book *The Seven Habits of Highly Effective Families,* Stephen Covey tells the story of two men cutting trees in the forest: one works hard all day long without a break while he notices the other taking frequent breaks during the day. As the day progresses, the one who stopped for breaks finishes the task and the tree comes down while the other is still slaving away at his job. So the first man asked, "What were you doing when you took those work breaks?" to which the second man replied, "I was sharpening my saw."[7]

When our priorities allow us to consciously take time for worship, for play, for work, for reflection, we are intentionally *sharpening our saws,* we are continually staying centered, keeping our lives and our marriage rightly ordered.

Benedict's Rule and the vows taken by the monks were based on the concept of balance. Benedict's instructions on finding balance in life—balance between work, prayer, and study—have been compared to a three-legged stool. If any one of the three legs is too short, the stool will wobble; if any leg is missing, the stool won't stand up.

If you've ever participated in individual spiritual direction, you know how valuable this balance is in life; however, it can become even more harmonious when practiced in the community of marriage or family as a corporate act. The balance of work, prayer, and study can also be thought of as a balance of body (work), spirit (prayer), and mind (study) or a truly holistic way of living well and holy—it not only makes sense, it is also the way God created us to live.

Finding balance in marriage and family does not mean compromise; rather, it is living with the end goal in focus, keeping equilibrium in the middle of the polarity of body, mind and spirit, and finding the presence of God at the center. Like that 33 1/3 LP, a marriage relationship in balance makes sweet and harmonious music. And like a balanced 3-legged stool, it can handle the pressures of life.

TAKING BACK YOUR FAMILY'S SABBATH REST

From the very beginning of the biblical account, God sets the stage for keeping a rhythm and balance in daily life. Genesis 2:3 says that, "God blessed the seventh day and made it holy, because on it he rested from all the work of creating that he had done."

---

7. Adapted from Covey, *Seven Habits of Highly Effective People,* 287.

In Isaiah 58:13 the prophet reminds the people of God that by keeping the Sabbath holy (or *wholly*) they would find their joy in the Lord.

The fourth commandment not only describes how best to live in community, in balance and stability; it also serves as a prescription for the health of the community, because if we don't keep the Sabbath as a day of rest from the labors of the other six days, we will surely die (Exod 31:12–18 and Jer 17:19–27). In other words, if you don't live according to the rhythm of life designed by God you will kill yourself from the stress (physical, mental, and emotional) that comes from living life out of balance!

While living in the Wheaton area, Dennis and I belonged to a group of couples who enjoyed lively book discussions. For one discussion our group decided to read a book by Marva Dawn, *Keeping the Sabbath Wholly: Ceasing, Resting, Embracing, Feasting.* After working our way through this book discussion, the couples in our group all agreed that this book moved us to change our own behavior more than any other book we'd read and discussed together up to that time. Why? Because although we are all involved in leadership roles of Christian service in various areas, we all knew that keeping the balance and commitment of Sabbath was hard to do and we were all equally convicted. After our reading and armed with a better understanding of the importance of intentionally keeping Sabbath, we all enjoyed the challenge of holding the others accountable.

So what does it actually mean to keep the Sabbath day holy? Dawn describes this as *ceasing* from the "incessant need to produce and accomplish, from all the anxieties about how we can be successful in all that we have to do to get ahead," in order to "let God be God in our lives."[8]

It is ceasing from all the buying and selling that cause us to think about what *we* want against God's desires for us. When we allow possessions to dominate our desires instead of longing for the presence of God we risk giving in to a character dominated

8. Dawn, *Keeping the Sabbath Wholly,* 29.

by materialism and perhaps even addictions. "We focus on what we will get out of a transaction instead of on the fact that God has given us all our money so that we can be generous toward others."[9]

Sabbath is ceasing from the enculturation of our marriage and family in order to realize our identity as God's Kingdom citizens. And it is ceasing from the humdrum and meaninglessness of life, for as Abraham Herschel points out, "the Sabbath is not for the sake of the weekdays; the weekdays are for the sake of Sabbath. It is not an interlude but the climax of living."[10]

Keeping the Sabbath day holy also means resting. "To give ourselves a day's break from emotional and intellectual problems enables us to come back to them with fresh perspectives, creative insights, and renewed spirits."[11] Intentionally setting aside one day each week is like having a mini-vacation for our physical bodies and for our souls. It counteracts the cultural emphasis on busyness and restlessness.

Keeping the Sabbath day holy means embracing, which means "we don't just think God's values are good. We embrace them *wholly*."[12]

Keeping the Sabbath day holy means that we practice Christian hospitality with grace (which I write about in the next chapter).

In an article for *USA Weekend*, Wayne Muller reminds us that:

> In the relentless busyness of modern life, we have lost the rhythm between action and rest. . . . The more our life speeds up, the more we feel weary, overwhelmed and lost. . . . [T]he whole experience of being alive begins to melt into one enormous obligation. It becomes the standard greeting everywhere: "I'm so busy." We say this

9. Ibid., 38.
10. Quoted in Ibid., 49.
11. Ibid., 52.
12. Ibid., 100.

to one another with no small degree of pride, as if our exhaustion were a trophy, our ability to withstand stress a mark of real character.[13]

Some practical ideas for keeping Sabbath in your home might include intentionally practicing the habit of a family meal each week and making it a more holy and meaningful experience for your family by adding candlelight or cloth napkins. Or invite others into your home after church services for a meal together as an act of hospitality, as well as holding your family accountable to Sabbath keeping. Perhaps the time could be spent verbally naming the ways God showed up during the past six days and recounting aloud your thankfulness.

Wayne Mueller also suggests an activity he calls "inviting a Sabbath Pause."[14] This is done by choosing one common act—touching a doorknob, turning on a faucet or hearing the phone ring, so that throughout the day when this common act occurs, you are reminded to stop and remember God's faithfulness in your life.

Another suggestion is to create a Sabbath box in your home.[15] Put your "to do" list, your keys, your wallet—anything you don't need in Sabbath time—into your box. Or write down a particular worry or concern and drop it in. Just for one day a week, let it go. Set aside a time on a Sabbath day to review your marriage mission statement and reevaluate how you are intentionally living toward your purpose and your goals.

By observing Sabbath in a regular rhythm you can be reminded that your marriage and your family move within a different reality. We are not human beings having occasional spiritual experiences; rather we might learn the reality of being spiritual beings having human experiences.

Defy what the culture tells you to be. As followers of God, we have a name, we have been chosen and set apart for a holy

13. Muller, "Remember the Sabbath?"

14. Ibid.

15. Ibid.

purpose (1 Pet 2:9–10). Sabbath-keeping is a way of finding balance in life and in relationships.

WHAT DO THESE STONES MEAN?

A few years ago our church family dedicated a new ministry facility. As part of that dedication each man, woman, and child was given a smooth stone and a permanent marker and encouraged to write something on that stone that identified them as a child of God and as a member of our community of faith. After writing on the stone, each person tossed or placed it gently into an open pit around the base of our St. Andrew's cross that stands in our church plaza. Our pastor told the Old Testament story of our ancestors in faith as Joshua led them through the Jordan River and into the Promised Land.

As the story goes in Joshua 4, after the Hebrew people had all crossed through the Jordan into the Promised Land, the Lord instructed twelve men, one from each of the tribes of Israel, to pick up a smooth stone from the bottom of the river bed and place them on the new land where it would serve as a sign among the people so that,

> In the future, when your children ask you, "What do these stones mean?" tell them that the flow of the Jordan was cut off before the ark of the covenant of the Lord. These stones are to be a memorial to the people of Israel forever. (Josh 4:6b–7)

As we placed the stones at our church, we were reminded and remembered our story in God's Story. We remembered that we are a people set apart for God's Kingdom purposes—"a chosen people, a royal priesthood, a holy nation, a people belonging to God" (1 Pet 2:9).

When we intentionally re-member our family in the rhythm of Sabbath worship and rest we become grounded and stable, finding the balance, wholeness, and holiness that God calls us to as a witness in the culture.

BEING RADICALLY ROOTED COUNTERACTS
A CULTURE OF FEAR

I cannot conclude this chapter without bringing up something else that works against peace, stability, and balance in our national ethos. Since the attack on our nation on September 11, 2001 we have all, as a nation, felt more vulnerable. This did not completely begin with the 9/11 attack; however, that event intensified the fears that had already become an undercurrent in our culture and gave rise to what is often referred to as a "culture of fear." Unfortunately, many of those we look to as leaders in our Christian community have exacerbated that fear by crediting attacks and even natural disasters to God's judgment.

There is no getting around the fact that we live in fear that completes or more often complements the other issues and values vying for our hearts and minds in our culture. Fear added to our national obsession with consumerism leads to guilt and hoarding in order to gain some semblance of security for our families and ourselves.

Fear added to hyper-individualism exacerbates hoarding and holding as the fear is manifested in a desire to protect what is ours and empowers us toward the current national tendency toward entitlement and obsession with our rights.

The physical and emotional effects of living within a constant tension of fear and anxiety feed our dependence on therapy and our desire to look even to the church and to God to make the world OK again.

Unfortunately the media, particularly what has been referred to as "talk radio," has often fed that fear, and some broadcasters have been accused of fear-mongering or unsettling listeners in a conscious or unconscious effort to boost ratings. A constant diet of media news and talk radio causes undue anxiety, mistrust, and anger even among our Christian marriages and families.

In a recent book, Michael Chabon writes in a chapter titled "The Lost Wilderness of Childhood" that

The endangerment of children—that persistent theme of
our lives, arts, and literature over the past twenty years—
resonates so strongly because, as parents, as members of
preceding generations, we look at the poisoned legacy
of modern industrial society and its ills, at the world
of strife and radioactivity, climatological disaster, over-
population, and commodification, and feel guilty. As the
national feeling of guilt over the extermination of the
Indians led to the creation of a kind of cult of the Indian,
so our children have become cult objects to us, too precious to be risked. At the same time they have become
fetishes, the objects of an unhealthy and diseased fixa-
tion. And once something is fetishized, capitalism steps
in and finds a way to sell it.[16]

In so doing, Chabon writes, we have closed down the wilderness
of the development of children's imagination.

Not only with our children, but possibly also with our marriages, we have lost our ability to assess risk. By worrying about
the wrong things, we often do damage to our children, raising
them to be anxious and unadventurous. We also do damage to
our marriage relationship by allowing our worry and our restlessness to deprive our relationship of a sense of corporate wonder and imagination. We control our vision of what we might
become together by our overwhelming consuming reaction to
guilt and anxiety.

When we assuage our guilt by consuming material possessions and media, not only are our children deprived of the confidence, experience and resourcefulness that come by having to
use their resources and their imagination to survive and thrive,
but we also deprive our marriage of the same confidence and
resourcefulness.

Fear has been likened to a kind of fungus: invisible, insidious, perfectly designed to decompose your peace of mind. Fear
of physical danger is at least subject to rational argument; fear
of failure is harder to rationalize. What could be more natural

16. Chabon, *Manhood for Amateurs*, 68.

than worrying that your child might be trampled by the great, scary, globally competitive world into which she will one day be launched?

Marjorie Thompson, writing in the mid-90s, reminded us that technological advances have led to exponential change at virtually every level of our lives. She pointed out that the rate of change over the past century has resulted in enormous social dislocation and stress. People are restless and longing for some center of stability and balance in their lives amid such rapid and pervasive change.[17]

In just the last fifteen years since Thompson's book was published, pervasive changes in technology have exploded and caused such social dislocation in our culture and around our world that, as we are barely learning to navigate our way through Internet, e-mail, cell phone, GPS systems, and all the other advances that wireless technology offers, we find ourselves face to face (literally) with Facebook, Twitter, and many other social networks vying for our time and attention. Add to that the tremendous impact and popularity of texting among youth and the words that Marjorie Thompson wrote a mere fifteen years ago take on even more meaning.

"We live in a culture that glorifies superficial values. As a society we have little deep sense of purpose that calls us to sacrifice individual desires for the sake of a larger good . . . We are beginning to starve for values of enduring substance." [18]

By seeking and finding balance in life—by putting God and a strong and foundational faith and faith heritage at the center of our marriage and family relationship; by slowing down our frenetic pace and guilty consumption; by intentionally taking back our family's Sabbath rest—we are in a better position to be radically rooted so that, as I said at the beginning of this chapter, our marriage and our families are able to stand firm within the social and cultural whirlwinds that sweep others off course.

17. Thompson, *Soul Feast*, 3.
18. Ibid.

CONVERSATION STARTERS

Focusing Outward: Habits to try on . . .

1. Discuss the advantages of living with the same person for a lifetime.

2. In what ways might we find ourselves in bondage if we are constantly changing partners or communities, or freed if we stay with the same person or community for the rest of our lives?

3. What is the difference between a "contractual marriage" and a "covenantal marriage"?

4. Set a three-month goal (twelve weeks) of "Sabbath Keeping" with your family. Spend time intentionally planning for success and reevaluate at the end of the three-month journey. Some suggestions for intentional planning:

   - What is our first priority for our Sabbath rest? How do we hold ourselves accountable? What is our desired outcome?

   - How can we avoid the temptations of shopping, acquiring, and catching up on business for a full day? What planning ahead activities are necessary to make it work?

   - How can we use our Sabbath as an opportunity to bless others in our family? Our church family? Our community?

Focusing Inward: Family Bible Talk . . .

1. Read the story of Joshua leading the Hebrew people into the Promised Land in the Old Testament book of Joshua.

   - What was the value of placing the stones on the new land? Where might your family decide to place stones as a reminder of God's call on your life?

   - How did those stones serve as a reminder to future generations? Was it seeing the stones or was it telling of stories of God's acts that gave the people a purpose?

   - In what ways did this physical and intentional act help develop a sense of identity and hope for the people?

9

Kitchen Community in a Garage Door Society

Re-Envisioning the Kingdom

What you do for God beyond your home will not typically be greater than what you practice with God within your home.

—G. Wishall

All guests who present themselves are to be welcomed as Christ, for he himself will say: I was a stranger and you welcomed me.

—Rule of St. Benedict 53.1

Above all, maintain constant love for one another, for love covers a multitude of sins. Be hospitable to one another without complaining. Like good stewards of the manifold grace of God, serve one another with whatever gift each of you has received.

1 Peter 4:8–10

When you have a stranger with two feet under your dining room table, you have them half way to the kingdom of God.

—Henrietta Mears

SEEING GOD'S KINGDOM LIVED "INSIDE-OUT" IN YOUR FAMILY

O NCE THERE WAS SOMEONE who said such amazing things and did such wonderful things that all the people began to follow him and wanted to hear all that he had to tell them. He talked a lot about the Kingdom, and the people asked what this Kingdom might really be and where this Kingdom might be found. And so he told them in parables, using places and stuff with which they were already familiar—so they could begin to imagine what this place called the Kingdom might really be.

One day as he began talking about the Kingdom of God, he picked up a seed in the garden and commented on how small the seed was. One could hardly imagine anything large growing from such a small seed. However, he told them, when the seed is planted in good soil and when it is watered and nourished, that tiny seed will begin to put down strong roots and break through the soil into the light. As I tell this story from *Godly Play*[1] to our church's children I place the seed in a bright yellow circle and cover it with a balled up "tree" of green felt which I slowly begin to unroll as I tell the parable. And as I open up the trunk and branches of the mustard seed tree I wonder aloud about Jesus telling this story of the Kingdom. I wonder, with the children, where this Kingdom might really be and I wonder how deep the roots must go to hold up such a large tree. I wonder how many branches the tree might have and if the branches might look inviting for the birds of the air to come and build their nests. When the tree is completely unfurled on the bright yellow circle of light I invite each child in our circle to come and place a nest in the branches and choose a unique bird to settle in their nest. Each bird is different—some are red and some are yellow, some or black and white and some are brown. As each child chooses his or her nest and bird I comment how each is different and I wonder if each might feel welcomed in the mustard seed tree. I

---

1. Berryman and Stewart, *Young Children and Worship.* 156–58.

wonder how many different kinds and colors of birds there might really be and if there is room for them all in the tree. Then I sit back and wonder again why Jesus told this parable to the people and what God's Kingdom might really be and if there might really be a place for everyone to come and make their home in God's Kingdom. Then we light our Christ Candle and read this parable from the Bible together and wonder a little bit more while some of the children reflect aloud on what Jesus really means about the Kingdom and how they might really belong to that wonderful Kingdom. We also wonder how God might ask us to make room for others in the Kingdom and who'd be welcomed there—even those who might be different from us.

Perhaps you can remember a time when you felt truly welcomed as a participant in Christ's church and God's Kingdom. Or perhaps an experience of connectedness that you knew held a deeper meaning in your life than simply being entertained. In this chapter on the discipline of hospitality, I want to draw your reflection to those special times in life when you knew that you were not only being welcomed—you knew that you belonged. Perhaps you can recall those opportunities in your married life when your family had welcomed others or been welcomed by others that have helped form you and allowed you opportunity to participate in God's Kingdom.

INTENTIONAL HOSPITALITY

Hospitality, when intentionally Kingdom-focused, is different from what the term hospitality usually connotes in our culture. We often equate hospitality with social occasions, with cooking fancy meals or using the good dishes and serving the meal in the dining room instead of eating in the kitchen. In fact, if you asked, most folks in our culture would say that entertaining and hospitality are synonymous. But Kingdom-focused hospitality is not necessarily synonymous with entertaining. There are many ways in which Christian hospitality is unique and can be an opportunity for Kingdom focus in our communities.

Think about this: the word "hospitality" has at its root in the Latin word *hospes,* which means "host." Hospitality is foundationally related to words and images such as *hospital, hospice, hostel* and *hotel.* By thinking about that, I am better able to understand the distinctions between entertaining and showing hospitality. In much the same way that a hospital or a hostel welcomes and provides for guests and cares for strangers and heals those in need, Kingdom-focused hospitality brings healing and provides for rest, regeneration, and renewal.

KINGDOM HOSPITALITY: A BIBLICAL MODEL

In the Bible, hospitality is not an accidental theme. It is a lifeline that runs through the whole of the ongoing story of God's people. Think of just a few familiar Bible stories: Abraham, who welcomed the strangers that turned out to be the very persons of God (Gen 18); Rahab, the woman of Jericho who welcomed the spies of Israel even though it meant risking her life (Josh 2); and Jesus, who welcomed sinners to eat with Him. "Hospitality inevitably makes us vulnerable to the stranger, whereas generosity does not."[2] Abraham, Rahab, and especially Jesus put their reputations and even their lives on the line in acts of hospitality; at the very least they were inconvenienced. These are more acts of *hospes* than *entertainment.* And there are others in our biblical family story: the widow who gave up her last meal to a stranger (1 Kings 17); the woman who gave water to a stranger at the Samaritan well (John 4); Boaz, who even went beyond the role of *hospes* and showed the Hebrew concept of *hesed*[3] to a foreigner— and not *just* a foreigner, but a despised and feared citizen of the nation of Moab (Ruth; also Deut 23). And "when Jesus sent out the twelve, instructing them not to carry extra money or clothing, he was issuing not only a call to these disciples to proclaim

---

2. Garland, *Family Ministry,* 356.

3. The Hebrew word *hesed* connotes *love growing out of a covenant beyond the call of duty.*

the good news but also a call to the community of believers to extend hospitality."[4] (See Mark 6.)

Hospitality has always been important for Christians. Not so incidentally, Christians were the ones who founded all of the aforementioned places of hospitality: *hospital, hospice*, and even the origins of *hostels*. It is interesting, though, that most hospitals, hostels, and hospice care have all grown into institutions that are no longer exclusively linked with the church.

I WAS A STRANGER AND YOU WELCOMED ME— ST. BENEDICT

St. Paul instructed the church in Rome to "welcome one another, as Christ has welcomed you" (Romans 15:7). The early Christian believers made it a habit to always welcome each other as Christ. And in the sixth century when St. Benedict wrote his rule of conduct for life, he included a vow of hospitality as a model of Christ-like discipline for his monks. Simply stated, the *Rule of St. Benedict* reminds us to receive each guest as if the guest were Jesus Christ himself coming into our midst. *"All guests who present themselves are to be welcomed as Christ, for he himself will say: I was a stranger and you welcomed me."* This vow, practiced so honestly and freely by the monks of Blue Cloud Abbey in Marvin, South Dakota, impressed my husband and his "mostly Baptist" students when they visited there; it impacted their lives in such a way that many of them felt God's calling for new directions in ministry.

HOSPITALITY AS A SPIRITUAL DISCIPLINE

True hospitality, in juxtaposition with entertaining, means not hiding who our family really is (be that the monastic family, church family, or nuclear family at home), but opening the family's boundaries to include the other (including perhaps the

4. Garland, *Family Ministry*, 355.

stranger or foreigner). "It means inviting another into the heart of the family as a valued representative of Christ's presence."[5]

Within our current culture, the specialization of hospitality through hospitals and hotels has, in some ways, taken this biblical practice away from the lives of ordinary Christians. Our lives, our families, and our congregations aren't really ordered in such a way that we can readily welcome a guest in the night or invite the hungry to share a meal.

But there are some model communities that give Christians who want to intentionally offer hospitality cause for hope. For instance, consider homeless shelters or special needs communities, which provide space for people with and without disabilities to live together. These can be enriching opportunities for families to practice hospitality in a somewhat controlled environment, especially for families with elementary aged children. When our children were young, for example, we practiced Christian hospitality as we visited folks without relatives in nursing homes or elder care facilities, or when we drove into the city of Chicago to take part in serving meals through ministries to people on the streets with Emmaus Ministry (mentioned in an earlier chapter of this book). When have you intentionally stepped outside the cultural expectations and experienced the richness (or sometimes the uncomfortable awkwardness) of showing *hospes* or even *hesed?* In our family we have experienced the act of hospitality beyond entertaining guests on a couple of occasions: one was inviting the Palestinian young man, that I mentioned in early chapters, to live with our family for a year while he attended graduate school. We met Yohana on a Wheaton College trip to Israel. We were able to be instrumental in his application and scholarship process, and, after all was approved I said to my husband, "Well, now that he's coming, he must have a place to stay. Let's invite him to live with us." The outcome was not only *hospes* for him, it was culturally and Christianly enriching for us and for our children, who were teenagers at the time. We experienced many other opportunities

5. Ibid., 355.

for Christian hospitality over the years: having a rich variety of houseguests and sharing meals around the dining table with a wealth of interesting characters. Our young children remember well coming downstairs early one morning to see a monk from Blue Cloud Abbey who had come to our home the night before, but well after they had gone to bed. Expecting to see a monk dressed in his "uniform," they found instead a fun and friendly guy wearing a T-shirt that said "Super Monk" across the front. One enriching experience in Christian hospitality surrounded our dinner table with a couple of Mormons, an Assembly of God minister, a Baptist minister and a couple of us Presbyterians. "For Christians, offering hospitality should be a vital part of our very identity. We are people who have been welcomed by someone no less than God Himself"[6] (see Luke 15).

Our good friends Robert and Elizabeth Roberts have been especially good models for us over the years by welcoming the stranger into their home. We know of a couple of incidents where it didn't appear to turn out so good for them—including taking in a supposedly recovering Moonie who was working the system. However, even that experience, in hindsight, served to be a means of enriching their family, their marriage, and their Christian witness in a way that it would not have been had they not been willing to risk. "Our Lord is the one who scandalized his people by sharing meals with the outcasts of his day—tax collectors and sinners. Our Lord is also the one who hosts us—and, many of us believe, feeds us his very own body—at our shared meal of Holy Communion. We are called to welcome the stranger as we would Jesus himself (Matt 25:40)."[7]

6. Ibid., 357.
7. Ibid., 356.

CREATING KINGDOM-STYLE HOSPITALITY
FOR THE FAMILY-LESS

Another beautiful opportunity for the vow of hospitality within the Christian home is the privilege of including the "family-less" within our church family. "The church bears responsibility for ensuring that no one in the family of faith is family-less—that everyone is folded into the nurture of family. God created humanity with a purpose, a mission of care."[8] In our American culture in the past few decades we have done a disservice to the Kingdom by creating what we call *family ministry* that caters only to the narrowly defined traditional family of father, mother, and children. I am challenged and delighted with the new paradigm of family ministry being championed by folks such as Diana Garland, Mark DeVries, Lee Cameron, and Timothy Paul Jones (to name a few) who are calling the local church to rethink the distinctions of family as well as to rethink how the church does ministry within the whole intergenerational faith community with folks in all ages and stages of life.

PARTY WITH JESUS:
INTENTIONALLY CELEBRATING THE RITUALS
AND RHYTHMS OF OUR CHURCH YEAR

"One of the ways families point to the good news is to celebrate our life as family together, as witness to the big party to come when the kingdom achieves its fullness."[9] Christian families show hospitality by being intentional about celebrating the rituals and rhythms of our church year calendar and our rich history and heritage of the Bible and the historical church. When a family celebrates the rituals and rhythms of the church year at home, the history and connection to the historical church becomes a means of being hospitable within the family home as it joins in celebration with the whole church community. In so doing, the rituals

8. Ibid., 373.
9. Ibid., 361.

and rhythms of our church year and the history of God's people become more meaningfully integrated into our daily lives.

For example, when an elementary aged child is baptized in our church family they participate in what we call our "young believer's baptism" ministry. We give each family a special candle with instructions to light the candle each year on the anniversary of the child's baptism. (I also suggest that they may want to use the same candle to light at their wedding to remind everyone present that they are connecting their new family with the family of faith.) Other opportunities of hospitality and celebration that witness to God's Kingdom might be to celebrate Advent or Lent in a special way within your family traditions; or celebrate the day of Pentecost (the birthday of the church!) with balloons and cupcakes, and invite your neighborhood to join in.

THE BOOKEND OF OUTWARD HOSPITALITY

Hospitality takes on an inner family focus for the Kingdom as well as an external focus. While we begin to recognize opportunities to welcome strangers and foreigners into our homes and fellowship, those who are blessed with children in their marriages might also recognize the opportunity to welcome those new little strangers into their family. As Diana Garland puts it, "Procreation actually is the other bookend to hospitality. If hospitality welcomes and enfolds others into the family, procreation blesses and sends out."[10] "We as earthly parents are given the privilege to be conduits of God's gracious work in our children's lives."[11]

Part of that hospitality to our own children is to graciously show both *hospes* and *hesed* as a faithful model from our brothers and sisters in the biblical story; we covenant with God to welcome them into our faith-family as much as our birth-family and nation-family. Celebrating the stories of faith, observing the

10. Ibid., 356.

11. Kang, "When Our Children Become Our Brothers, Sisters, and Friends in God's Household."

calendar of the church year, and participating in externally-focused, Kingdom-focused hospitality forms our children as well as ourselves and it holds the means of blessing and sending our children out into the world.

The goal of all Christian hospitality is transformation into the perfect familial fellowship in the Kingdom of God. "The necessity of hospitality [in our Christian community] converts our homes from insulated havens into adventurous mission bases. Hospitality gives families a purpose beyond themselves. They exist to serve God and the world through the church."[12]

The way that we participate in the celebration and hospitality of other children in our family of faith also enriches God's Kingdom and promotes a Kingdom mission purpose. I think of the many people in my faith journey who have shown me hospitality as I grew up in faith as a child, youth, young adult, wife, and mother. A particularly meaningful witness to the Kingdom for us was a divorced woman who took us under her wing as twenty-something graduate students with a first child. Marian Cross has been the fodder of sermons that my husband has preached on grace and forgiveness. Marian was also a model of hospitality to both of us over the years, adopting us into her motley family made up of several single adults, some widows, a few seminary students, and the like. Many *hospes* as well as a couple of *hesed* moments stick in my mind as I think of Marian's model of Kingdom-focused grace.

One time, in particular, we were enjoying conversation over coffee in her perfectly manicured home with a fine wood coffee table and white carpet. Our toddler son, Ryan, was playing on the living room floor as we talked and, in an instant, rammed his toy truck into the coffee table, upsetting the coffee cups and sending coffee spilling over the table (there went the wood finish) and onto the white carpet. Marian's immediate response was one of grace and a defining moment in my understanding of hospitality. She immediately exclaimed, "Oh my, now every time I look at

12. Clapp, *Families at the Crossroads*, 162.

that coffee stain I will be able to remember my precious Ryan!"
Hospitality is a means of showing grace, and I will never, ever
forget the grace that was freely given and received that day. *Hesed*
hospitality is showing grace that can move us beyond entertaining and caring about appearances to real Kingdom fellowship
both within and outside of our normal comfort zone. It takes
practice and prayer and intentional seeking for opportunities to
be Christ in our world.

SEEING OTHERS AS CHRIST

As I mentioned earlier in this chapter, St. Benedict added the
vow of hospitality to his *Rule* as a means of spiritual discipline
for his monks. Above the door of many Benedictine monasteries
you will likely see a sign posted that says, "All guests who present
themselves are to be welcomed as Christ."[13] The monks are taught
to see each guest, no matter their reason for coming nor their
station in life, as Christ himself in their midst. A practice to help
you begin to accomplish this spiritual discipline of hospitality in
your home, your church, your work, as well as to the person on
the sidewalk or on the train or freeway on your way to work,
might be to picture each person as though Christ was standing
beside or behind that person, or riding in the car alongside that
person.

What would it mean in your daily interactions if you saw
Jesus Christ standing behind the person with whom you work?
Or the person waiting on you at the supermarket, or standing
behind your spouse? What would it mean if you could picture
Christ standing behind the person you find it most difficult to
like?

In his book *Monk Habits*, Dennis says that it would be
interesting if the incarnation had taken place in twenty-first-
century North America instead of first century Palestine. Jesus
may have been as poorly received by and unattractive to our

13. RB, 53.1.

mega-churches as he was in the "mega-synagogues" and temple of his own people. After all, we'd have to extend the right hand of fellowship to a homeless man who had a reputation for hobnobbing with the winebibbers and tax collectors. At best, we might show him hospitality as one of our "see-how-we-minister-to-the-poor" trophies. I remember a school semester when Dennis decided, in the spirit of Benedict, to pray each morning, "Lord, send someone today whom I can serve." But he confesses that he decided to give up the practice because inevitably that someone would show up five minutes before he had to dash out the door to deliver a lecture or when he was on his way out the door for a quick lunch.[14]

KEEPING YOUR MARRIAGE STUCK
AND YOUR FAMILY STICKY

Another Kingdom focus for hospitality is to remember how Christ welcomes us to his table regularly in the act of communion in our church community. In his book *It Takes a Church to Raise a Christian,* Tod Bolsinger talks about seeing the table in your kitchen, conference room, or dining room as Christ's communion table.

> Whether it be a kitchen table where a friend shares a burden over coffee, a boardroom table where a company's strategic plans are confirmed, or a courtroom table where justice is sought, to the Christian these tables can become "communion tables" where Jesus' own inclusive love is offered. Our responsibility is to have the mindset of a servant, representing Christ, who is always, though often unacknowledged, the host of the gathering and the one inviting every person into the life-transforming communion."[15]

As families practice hospitality together and serve together they discover a deeper understanding of one another and of God.

14. Okholm, *Monk Habits*, 87.
15. Bolsinger, *It Takes a Church*, 163.

They find their faith more resilient and meaningful. The children in those families develop what Eric Swanson and Diana Garland have coined a "sticky faith,"[16] a faith that helps to keep families of all generations "stuck" to the church and faith in God as they walk through life. Faith lived out in actions of service and hospitality gives families a grounding that carries them through the crises and deep struggles that life inevitably holds, and empowers them to live more within the biblical purpose and biblical story of God's faithful people. "Once you were not a people, but now you are the people of God; once you had not received mercy but now you have received mercy" (1 Pet 2:10, NIV).

As a people of God and as participants in His Kingdom purpose for the world, our response and our identity is not only to receive grace and mercy; our identity as God's people comes when we participate in and extend grace, mercy, and hospitality to all and see others as Christ in our midst.

CONVERSATION STARTERS

Focusing Outward: Habits to try on . . .

1. Try this: picture Jesus Christ standing behind your spouse, or your child or parent, or behind the person with whom you work, or the person you find it most difficult to like. How would this change your words and/or actions? Why?

2. What keeps me/us from sincerely praying, "Lord, send someone I/we can serve today?"

Focusing Inward: Family Bible Talk . . .

Reread some of the Biblical stories of hospitality and put yourself into the story, how would you react? What difference would it have made for God's Kingdom at that point

---

16. Garland, *Inside Out Families,* 11.

in time if you were the one who had to choose to extend hospitality or not?

1. Abraham and the unexpected guests (Gen 18)

   - Would you invite these strangers into your home? Why or why not?

   - How would you have responded to their announcement?

2. Boaz and the widow (Ruth)

   - If this stranger from a foreign nation with which you had been at war appeared in your community, gleaning (or begging) at your establishment, how might you treat her? How might you see her: as someone to value and assist or as someone to be tolerated?

   - Do you wonder why Boaz treated her this way? What knowledge or worldview did he have that caused him to act as he did?

3. The people living in the villages visited by the disciples of Jesus (Mark 6)

   - Putting yourself into the place of the villagers, how might you have interacted with these disciples of Jesus?

   - Putting yourself in the place of the disciples, how would you feel? How would you follow the instructions of Jesus?

4. Rahab, who risked opening her home to the Hebrew spies (Josh 2)

   - Rahab put her life on the line for these strangers/enemies. Why? What would you have done?

- What caused her to have such wisdom and foresight? (NOTE: Rahab was the mother of Boaz in the Ruth story.)

5. The feeding of the 5,000 by Jesus (Mark 8)

   - If you had been the disciples in this story, what would you have done? Would you have trusted Jesus or would you have doubted?

   - If you had been the little boy with what appeared to be the only food around, would you have been willing to give your lunch away to Jesus or would you have preferred to keep it for yourself? Why is this such a remarkable story even beyond the miracle?

Bibliography

Archer, Harris, et al. *Theological Wordbook of the Old Testament*. Chicago: Moody, 1980.

Bakke, Ray. http://cityvoices.gospelcom.net/pages/raybakke/ray_apstle.html.

Barna, George. *The Second Coming of the Church: A Blueprint for Survival*. Nashville: Nelson, 1998.

————. www.barna.org/barna-update/article/15-familykids/42-new-marriage -and-divorce-statistics-released.

Barrett, Mike. "Searching for Radical Faith." *Christianity Today*, February 27, 2009. http://www.christianitytoday.com/ct/2009/february/30.36html.

Bartholomew, Craig, and Michael Goheen. *The Drama of Scripture: Finding Our Place in the Biblical Story*. Grand Rapids: Baker, 2004.

Barton, S. C. "Towards a Theology of the Family." *Christian Perspectives on Sexuality and Gender*. Edited by A. Thatcher and E. Stuart. Grand Rapids: Eerdmans, 1996.

Batchelder, David B. "The Home as Family Church." *Reformed Liturgy and Music*: Vol. 29.3, 165–72.

Bellah, Robert, et al. *Habits of the Heart: Individualism and Commitment in American Life*. Berkeley: University of California Press, 1996.

Bergler, Thomas E. "I Found My Thrill: The Youth for Christ Movement and American Congregational Singing, 1940–1970." *Wonderful Words of Life*. Edited by Richard J. Mouw and Mark A. Noll, 123–49. Grand Rapids: Eerdmans, 2004.

Berryman, Jerome, and Sonja Stewart. *Young Children in Worship*. Louisville: Westminster/John Knox, 1990.

Blankenhorn, David. *Fatherless America: Confronting Our Most Urgent Social Problem*. New York: Basic, 1995.

Bolsinger, Tod. *It Takes a Church to Raise a Christian: How the Community of God Transforms Lives*. Grand Rapids: Brazos, 2004.

Bronson, Po, and Ashley Merryman. *NurtureShock: New Thinking About Children*. New York: Hachette, 2009.

Brueggemann, Walter. *Finally Comes the Poet: Daring Speech for Proclamation*. Minneapolis: Augsburg Fortress, 1989

Burns, Erin. "Prayers for My Angels." September 15, 2008. http://www .bringingupburns.com/2008/09/prayers-for-my-angels.html.

Campolo, Tony. *Traditions: The Key to a Close Knit Family*. Podcast: January 1, 2000. http://podcast.christianaudio.com/?p=14.

Bibliography

Castleman, Robbie. *Parenting in the Pew: Guiding Your Children into the Joy of Worship*. Downer's Grove, IL: InterVarsity, 2002.

Chabon, Michael. *Manhood for Amateurs: The Pleasures and Regrets of a Husband, Father, and Son*. New York: Harper, 2009.

Cherlin, Andrew. "The Deinstitutionalization of American Marriage." *Journal of Marriage and Family* 66, November 2004, 846-861.

———. *The Marriage-Go-Round: The State of Marriage and the Family in America Today*. New York: Vintage, 2010.

Claiborne, Shane. *The Irresistible Revolution: Living as an Ordinary Radical*. Grand Rapids: Zondervan, 2006.

Claiborne, Shane, et al. *A Liturgy for Ordinary Radicals*. Grand Rapids: Zondervan, 2010.

Clapp, Rodney. *Families at the Crossroads: Beyond Traditional and Modern Options*. Downers Grove, IL: InterVarsity, 1993.

Coontz, Stephanie. *Marriage, a History: How Love Conquered Marriage*. New York: Penguin, 2006.

———. "Too Close for Comfort." *New York Times Magazine*. November 7, 2006. http://www.nytimes.com/2006/11/07/opinion/07coontz.html.

Covey, Stephen R. *First Things First: Coping with the Ever-Increasing Demands of the Workplace*. New York: Simon & Schuster, 1996.

———. *The Seven Habits of Highly Effective People*. New York: Simon & Schuster, 2004.

Craik, Laura. "Credit Crunch Shopping: Because I'm Worth It, Even When I'm Stony Broke . . ." MAILonline. May 20, 2008. http://www.dailymail.co.uk/femail/article-1020465/Credit-crunch-shopping-Because-Im-worth--Im-stony-broke-.html.

Dawn, Marva. *Keeping the Sabbath Wholly: Ceasing, Resting, Embracing, Feasting*. Grand Rapids: Eerdmans, 1989.

DeGraaf, John. *Affluenza*. Oley, PA: Bull Frog Films, 2005.

Dixon, Leslie. *Rites of Passage I*. www.birdsnbeesconnection.com.

Dobson, James. *Preparing for Adolescence*. Ventura, CA: Gospel Light, 2005.

Fannin, B. Kathleen. "Strength in Meekness," *Cows in Church*. Lima, OH: CSS Publishing, 1999.

Fry, Timothy, editor. *RB 1980: The Rule of St. Benedict*. Collegeville, MN: Liturgical, 1981.

Garland, Diana. *Family Ministry: A Comprehensive Guide*. Downer's Grove, IL: InterVarsity, 2000.

———. *Inside-Out Families: Living the Faith Together*. Waco, TX: Baylor University Press, 2010.

———. *Sacred Stories of Ordinary Families*. San Francisco: Jossey-Bass, 2003.

Gies, Francis, and Joseph Gies. *Marriage and Family in the Middle Ages*. New York: Harper & Row, 1987.

Glenn, Joshua. "Fake Authenticity." Issue 15 (1999). www.hermenaut.com.

Goodman, Barak, director. *Merchants of Cool*. Frontline/PBS Home Videos, 2005.

Bibliography

Groome, Thomas. *Christian Religious Education: Sharing our Story and Vision.* San Francisco: Harper & Row, 1980.

Hahn, Scott. *Christ and the Church: A Model for Marriage.* Excerpted from the transcript of Scott Hahn's audio and videotape presentation, "Christ and the Church: A Model for Marriage" as it appears in the "Catholic Adult Education on Video Program" with Scott and Kimberly Hahn. http://ww.nd.edu/~afreddos/courses/264/modmar.htm.

Hauerwas, Stanley. *The Peaceable Kingdom.* Notre Dame: University of Notre Dame Press, 1983.

Hauerwas, Stanley, and William Willimon. *Resident Aliens: Life in the Christian Colony.* Nashville: Abingdon, 1989.

———. *The Truth about God: The Ten Commandments in Christian Life.* Nashville: Abingdon, 1999.

Hays, Richard. *The Moral Vision of the New Testament.* San Francisco: Harper-San Francisco, 1996.

Hill, Penny. *Parenting for Life.* Tucker, GA: Parenting for Life Ministries, 1997.

Kang, S. Steve. "When Our Children Become Our Brothers, Sisters, and Friends in God's Household." *Priscilla Papers* 23.3 (Summer 2009) 14–17.

Kang, S. Steve, and Gary Perrott. *Teaching the Faith, Forming the Faithful: A Biblical Vision for Education in the Church.* Downers Grove, IL: InterVarsity, 2009.

Keeley, Robert. *Helping Our Children Grow in Faith.* Grand Rapids: Baker Books, 2008.

Kimball, Dan. *The Emerging Church: Vintage Christianity in a New Generation.* Grand Rapids: Zondervan/YS, 2003.

Kohlberg, Lawrence, et al. *Moral Development, Moral Education, and Kohlberg.* Birmingham: Religious Education Press, 1980.

Lee, Cameron. *Beyond Family Values: A Christian Call to Virtue.* Downer's Grove, IL: InterVarsity, 1998.

Lewis, C. S. *The Screwtape Letters.* New York: Harper Collins, 2001.

Lloyd-Jones, Sally. *The Jesus Storybook Bible: Every Story Whispers His Name.* Grand Rapids: ZonderKids, 2007.

Muller, Wayne. *Sabbath: Finding Rest, Renewal, and Delight in Our Busy Lives.* New York: Bantam, 2000.

National Center on Addiction & Substance Abuse at Columbia University. www.casacolumbia.org/absolutenm/templates/Home.aspx.

Nelson, C. Ellis. *Growing Up Christian: A Congregational Strategy for Nurturing Disciples.* Macon, GA: Smyth & Helwys, 2008.

Nile Theological College. www.pcusa.org/worldwide/globaled/nile.htm.

Novelli, Michael. *Shaped By The Story: Helping Students Encounter God in a New Way.* Grand Rapids: Zondervan/YS. 2008.

Okholm, Dennis. *Monk Habits: Benedictine Spirituality for Everyday People.* Grand Rapids: Brazos, 2007.

Okholm, Dennis, and Timothy Phillips. *A Family of Faith.* Grand Rapids: Baker Books, 2001.

Orvell, Miles. *The Real Thing: Imitation and Authenticity in American Culture, 1880–1940.* Chapel Hill, NC: 1989.

Parrott, Les and Leslie. *Becoming the Parent You Want to Be: Who You Are Matters More Than What You Do.* Grand Rapids: Zondervan, 2007.

Penner, Marv. *Youth Worker's Guide to Parent Ministry.* Grand Rapids: Zondervan, 2003.

Peterson, Eugene. *A Long Obedience in the Same Direction: Discipleship in an Instant Society.* Downer's Grove, IL: InterVarsity, 2000.

Prosser, Bo. "What Is the Missional Family?" *Center for Family and Community Ministries, Baylor Social Work.* Baylor University, 2009.

Rehm, Diane. The Diane Rehm Show. May 28, 2009. http://thedianerehmshow .org/shows/2009-05-28/andrew-cherlin-marriage-go-round-knopf.

Rinkert, Martin. "Now Thank We All Our God." Circa 1636, first appeared in *Praxis Pietatis Melica,* by Johann Cruger (Berlin, Germany: 1647). Translated from German to English by Catherine Winkworth, 1856.

Ritchie, James. *Always in Rehearsal: The Practice of Worship and the Presence of Children.* Nashville: Discipleship Resources, 2005.

Robinson, David. *The Family Cloister: Benedictine Wisdom for the Home.* New York: Crossroad, 2000.

Rusaw, Rick, and Eric Swanson. *The Externally Focused Church.* Loveland, CO: Group, 2004.

Selim, Ali, director. *Sweetland.* Adapted from Weaver, Will. *A Gravestone Made of Wheat.* 2005.

Smith, Christian, with Denton, Melinda Lundquist. *Soul Searching: The Religious and Spiritual Lives of American Teenagers.* Oxford: Oxford University Press, 2009.

Strommen, Merton P. "Rethinking Family Ministry." Ed. David S. Schuller, *Rethinking Christian Education.* Atlanta, GA: Chalice, 1993.

Stroup, George. *The Promise of Christian Narrative: Recovering the Gospel in the Church.* Atlanta: Westminster/John Knox, 1981.

Taylor, Brian. *Spirituality for Everyday Living: An Adaptation of the Rule of St. Benedict.* Collegeville, MN: Liturgical, 1989.

Thomas, David. *Christian Marriage: The New Challenge.* Collegeville, MN: Liturgical, 2007.

Thomas, Gary. *Sacred Marriage: What if God Designed Marriage to Make Us Holy More than to Make Us Happy?* Grand Rapids: Zondervan, 2000.

———. *Sacred Parenting: How Raising Children Shapes Our Souls.* Grand Rapids: Zondervan, 2004.

Thompson, Marjorie. *Family as the Forming Center: A Vision of the Role of Family in Spiritual Formation.* Nashville: Upper Room, 1996.

———. *Soul Feast: An Invitation to the Christian Spiritual Life.* Louisville: Westminster/John Knox, 1995.

Tournier, Paul. *To Understand Each Other.* Translated by John S. Gilmour. Richmond, VA: Westminster/John Knox, 1971.

Bibliography

Voskamp, Ann. *One Thousand Gifts: A Dare to Live Fully Right Where You Are.* Grand Rapids: Zondervan, 2011.

Walker, Ben. "More Than Fun and Games." *Christian Standard,* November 30, 2008. http://christianstandard.com/2008/11/cs_article-1059.

Waltke, Bruce. *The Way of Wisdom from the Book of Proverbs.* Vancouver, BC: Regent Audio, 2002.

Wangerin, Walter. *The Book of God: The Bible as a Novel.* Grand Rapids: Zondervan, 1996.

The Week. April 11, 2008. http://theweek.com/archive/2008/4.

————. January 29, 2010. http://theweek.com/archive/2010/1.

Wisdom, Alan F. H. "Is Marriage Worth Defending? Part II." *Theology Matters* 16.2 (March/April, 2010) 1–16.

Wuthnow, Robert, editor. *"I Come Away Stronger": How Small Groups are Shaping American Religion.* Grand Rapids: Eerdmans, 2001.

————. *Sharing the Journey: Support Groups and America's New Quest for Community.* New York: Free Press, 1994.